PRAISE FOR THE CALM & HAPPY HOME

"This book radiates with vibrant energy, guiding readers to transform their spaces into sanctuaries of balance and flow. It's full of practical wisdom, and I especially love the important insight into making children's bedrooms safe and peaceful, as that is absolutely vital. The book feels refreshingly modern and intuitive. It's a must-read for anyone ready to shift the energy in their home and their family's life."

- Jo Frost, parenting expert from TVs 'Supernanny'

"Kimberley stands among the UK's finest feng shui practitioners. This book is a masterclass in making your home work for you."

- Grant Pierrus, CEO and Founder of Interior Style Hunter, the award-winning luxury interior design blog

"In The Calm and Happy Home, *Kimberley has a true gift for making Feng Shui feel approachable rather than overwhelming. Her gentle guidance encouraged me to start small, and I'm already enjoying the sense of balance from simple steps like decluttering small spaces and opening my front door each morning to welcome fresh energy."*

- Sophie Webb, home organiser 'What Sophie Does'

"As someone who truly believes in the power of a calm and clutter-free home, The Calm and Happy Home *by Kimberley Gallagher completely spoke to my heart. It's not just a guide, it's a personal story of transformation, written with warmth, honesty and humour. This book shows how your home can support your energy, mindset and dreams in the most powerful way. I love how it makes Feng Shui feel relatable and modern, with practical steps anyone can take, no matter where you live or what your home looks like. A must read if you want your space to work with you, not against you."*

- Nicola Lewis, aka This Girl Can Organise (author, professional organiser and creator)

FENG SHUI MAGIC

What has Feng Shui helped you with?

I used the Northwest of my home to manifest a trip to the Maldives - and it happened!

My daughter used your tips in the West of her home especially as she was struggling to conceive - she is now expecting a baby!

I decluttered my wealth area and made a wealth bowl and added some money and a lottery ticket. I got £10k totally unexpected from a great uncle who had died over a year before and no inclination or any idea he would have thought about me, and a random tax rebate for £1400

I used the Rising Phoenix and wrote my intentions on the back of it - I received £40K of grant funding for my Community Interest Company!

With your Feng Shui guidance, manifesting and setting intentions, our son was accepted into a prestigious college for Year 7. It has been his dream and we are so happy!

After my analysis, my bank called to say we would be compensated for the bank closing and switching our mortgage - cheque in the post the next day!

Both my daughters got jobs!

THE CALM AND HAPPY HOME

Constant small money wins, money off shopping, credits on bills, not charged for parking, so much more!

My sense of hope has gone through the roof since using Feng Shui - it was like setting a re-set button on the house.

My house sold days after placing the brochure with SOLD written across it and placing it in the West of our home

I used Feng Shui in our health area and my husband is now in remission from prostate cancer

Feng Shui has been a blessing to my family and I - things are so much better in our home

WEALTH - my husband and I have both been crazy about cleaning our stove and we have both had massive pay increases and inheritance come our way

I made a wishlist of what I want in a new home and put it in the Northwest area - 2 weeks later we got our dream home

You mentioned something one day about mirrors and how they amplify what they reflect - my husband was MISERABLE in his job where he had been for 10 years, working all hours. Lightbulb moment - in his home office, he sat with his back facing a large mirror. I covered it up, said nothing to him and a couple of weeks later he applied for a new job completely out of the blue and got the job! And is now working much better hours, better communication and less stress too. I can't tell him it's because of the mirror, but it 100% is the reason!!!

FENG SHUI MAGIC

My dream job arrived just after I placed an affirmation in the South-East of my home - magic!

Stopped arguing so much with my husband!

My husband got his dream job with a great offer!

I tied a red ribbon under my sink and cleaned my stove with intention. I got a £400 tax refund

Out twins got into the same university - that was a dream come true and totally unexpected

A happier and calmer husband and he has no idea why!

I received £159 and £353 from unexpected credit after I added a money plant and a citrine crystal to the Southeast of my home

Immediately won £300 on the premium bonds and a client paid $500 debt he owed for months

We WON our dream home after manifesting a win on the home lottery in our wealth area and the rising phoenix

A good friend of mine found love again after much heartache - wedding next weekend!

I've been selling commissioned artworks on a regular basis since implementing Feng Shui

I got engaged and had a baby!

THE CALM & HAPPY HOME

WATKINS
1893

KIMBERLEY GALLAGHER

THE
CALM &
HAPPY
HOME

HOW TO BRING GOOD VIBES
INTO YOUR HOME & LIFE

The Calm & Happy Home

By Kimberley Gallagher

The first edition published in the UK and USA in 2025 by Watkins, an imprint of Watkins Media Limited, Unit 11, Shepperton House, 83–93 Shepperton Road, London N1 3DF

enquiries@watkinspublishing.com

Editorial Director: Ella Chappell
Commissioning Editor: Fiona Robertson
Managing Editor: Daniel Culver
Development Editor: Sophie Blackman
Editorial Assistant: Caitlin Nolan
Designer: Sneha Alexander
Head of Production: Uzma Taj

Interior Designed and Typeset by Sneha Alexander

Printed and bound by CPI Group (UK) Ltd, Croydon, CR0 4YY

The manufacturer's authorised representative in the EU for product safety is: eucomply OÜ - Pärnu mnt 139b-14, 11317 Tallinn, Estonia, hello@eucompliancepartner.com, www.eucompliancepartner.com

A CIP record for this book is available from the British Library

ISBN: 978-1-83681-011-7 (Hardback)

ISBN: 978-1-83681-019-3 (eBook)

10 9 8 7 6 5 4 3 2

www.watkinspublishing.com

CONTENTS

Part Three – Embrace the Feng Shui Lifestyle

REWRITING THE RULES: A FRESH APPROACH TO FENG SHUI

My Feng Shui Journey

If I asked you to describe your home, what words would you use? You might say something like, it's an apartment, it's a little cottage, it's a townhouse, it's a new build. You may even explain where it's located.

Have you ever considered that your home has its own personality? If you were to describe it, what characteristics would stand out? Would it be warm, friendly and supportive, or is it cold, dull, chaotic or even sad?

If you'd asked me five years ago if I thought my home had a personality, I probably would have thought you were going a little bit mad. However, over the last five years, things have changed quite a lot in the world and it was during lockdown that I first started to become aware of the energy inside my home. Like the majority of people around the world, I was at home 23 hours a day (with an hour allowed outside for exercise), so I got to know my home pretty well and I felt it had its own personality.

My home in the UK was in Surrey. It was a beautiful cottage built in 1569 and it was made from huge blocks of natural limestone. It was located in the countryside, had gorgeous cottage-style oak windows and doors, and was so lovely. Nevertheless, it did feel like it was almost stuck in its ways, and a little bit stubborn. We used to laugh all the time because we were forever trying to update the home to "modern times". We weren't asking for a lot, but it would have been nice to have had decent wi-fi and a heating system with a thermostat! I'm sure the electricians used to dread getting a phone call from us. There was always something that made the process of modernizing our home harder than it should have been.

During lockdown we were really reliant upon our home, not only to keep us safe and secure but also from a technological point of view as my daughter was home-schooled and I was trying to run a business. Put it this way, we couldn't be on social media at the same time as being on a video call! So, not only were we dealing with the technological side of things, but I was also trying to keep the home as calm as possible in what was quite a stressful, depressing time. My husband went out to work every day, which meant I was at home with my daughter and our dog every day, which got to me. And because of that I was searching and scraping around for anything and everything that I could do to keep the house calm.

I knew that keeping the place tidy was going to help. I knew that lighting a candle made me happy and I knew that I had to tackle the piles of laundry waiting for me to wash and put away as it was going to drain my energy if I had to look at it all day! So, I was doing all of those things. But keeping the home calm and positive was like fighting a constant battle, especially when the news was a never-ending stream of information that wasn't exactly uplifting. In fact, it was very negative and I knew it was beginning to impact my mental health. The saying "tidy house, tidy mind" really resonated with me and so I tried as hard as I could to keep everything tidy in the hope it would help me.

Because of this, I made a conscious decision to control the information that I was surrounding myself with. I stopped watching the news and having the TV on and instead listened to the Chris Evans Breakfast Show on Virgin Radio. I remember Chris talking about the fact that he believed in affirmations, would meditate and exercise daily, and listen to educational podcasts. He would come on the air every morning, bright as a button, beaming rays of light into everybody's homes. I wanted to be as happy as he was, so I copied pretty much everything he did.

I then stumbled across a podcast where there was a Feng Shui consultant talking about how you can use your home to attract a partner in your life. If I'm honest, the first thing I thought was *"What a load of nonsense!"* I had heard about Feng Shui, but I couldn't have told you what it entailed, and I definitely didn't understand the depth of Feng Shui. I thought it was just about aesthetics, having beautiful white furniture and perhaps a lucky cat somewhere in your home!

How Feng Shui Changed My Life

Seeing as I had quite a bit of time on my hands, I did some research and I found that a lot of hotels, shopping centres and airports around the world use Feng Shui principles to bring them wealth, prosperity and abundance. They do this because it creates a happier and calmer environment for their clients, who spend more money as a result. Many of the most successful entrepreneurs from around the world are also known to apply Feng Shui to their businesses because its aim is to create an environment that boosts productivity, brings wealth and success, and reduces stress.

I made it my mission to have my home "Feng Shui'd" and contacted the lady who was on the podcast to analyse my home in December 2020. I didn't really know what this meant, but I knew that she used the Five Elements (Fire, Wood, Earth, Metal and Water) in the home to get rid of the energy blocks, absorb any negative energy and make the positive energy flow. And that was all the information I needed to make my decision.

It was basically acupuncture for the home. If you've never had it, acupuncture works by stimulating specific points along the body's energy pathways with tiny needles (don't worry, they don't hurt) to help unblock and balance your energy. Instead of needles, Feng Shui uses the five elements, and I can honestly say that within a month of the elements being in my home, there was a huge energy shift. Some of the items I needed seemed absolutely bonkers, like 30kg (66lb) of metal in various areas of my home! But then other things were a lot subtler and easier to incorporate – for example, adding red decorative items to represent the Fire element or placing crystals to represent the Earth element. But who was I to question it? And I'm so glad I didn't because as mad as it sounds, the house became calmer and happier, and we somehow got our sense of humour back. We were also communicating with each other so much better.

The other magical thing that happened was my business. Before lockdown, I had had a feeling that I was going to be made redundant from my teaching role, so I started a business selling health and wellness products in February 2020 (great timing, I know!). A year into running this business, no matter what I did or which avenue I tried, I felt like I was banging my head against a brick wall. I was learning new skills. I was doing training courses on how to sell products online. I was messaging people left, right, and centre and I was manifesting as hard as I possibly could. There were sticky notes posted everywhere in the house with the amounts of money that I wanted to make! Hand on heart, I really did give it my best shot.

The Missing Part of the Manifestation Puzzle

Feng Shui and manifestation go hand in hand because both entail intentionally shaping your environment to align with your goals and desires. Manifestation is about attracting what you want, and Feng Shui focuses on creating the right energy flow to support it, which therefore intensifies the manifestation process. For me, this could not have been more true. One of the first steps in manifestation is being clear about what you want. Yet clarity is hard to find when you're surrounded by mess, distractions or things that no longer serve you.

My intentions were to have "any business" that allowed me to work completely remotely and with lovely people all around the world. I wanted to help people because that was really important to me, but I also wanted to be financially independent. A month after the elements and intentions went in, I received an email from the lady who Feng Shui'd my home to say that she was doing a certification course, possibly her last one, and asking if I would be interested in doing it. I felt that this was a massive message from whoever it was out there to say, "This is your pathway", even though just one month earlier I didn't really know what Feng Shui was! You can now imagine the awkward conversation I had with my husband about this investment because I hadn't even told him that I had Feng Shui'd our home! Although he did laugh out loud, he was amazing and said that I should do it and we would work it out. I told him that I'd pay him back even though I had no idea how, but I knew I would. I put my name down to do the course and I'm sure you can see by now, it was one of the best decisions that I've ever made in my life.

A Modern Approach to Feng Shui

I gave the course everything. I lived and breathed Feng Shui. It was almost like learning a new language because the way I saw buildings wasn't just about how they looked; I could see how well energy flowed. I had never come across anything like this before and it excited me. I could look at floor plans and evaluate whether people in certain rooms might struggle due to the location of their bedrooms. And all I could think of was how amazing it would be to help other people create beautiful, calm homes filled with love and laughter.

It became apparent during the course that everything was taught following the traditional Feng Shui methods and ideology. Of course it was. Feng Shui is over 4,000 years old and not much has changed in the teaching methods and practices, and so we learned about certain items that could be added to the home to increase wealth, health and relationships. For example, to attract wealth in your life, you could place a lucky cat in a certain area of your home, or you could have a wealth jar. You can even collect soil from prosperous homes that you have visited. And I thought, well, that's amazing, but it just isn't for us. If I put something like a bowl of soil from prosperous homes in our wealth area, it just wouldn't look right and also, if I'm honest, it wouldn't mean a lot to me either.

As the course went on, I knew that as a family we weren't quite ready to bring in these traditional methods, I needed to find a way to raise the vibrations in my home, in a way that fitted with modern-day living. And that's when I realized that to be able to help my friends and family, I needed to create a way of bridging the gap between these beautiful ancient practices and contemporary Western living.

Of course, not all homes need a full analysis to shift the energy; some homes only need little tweaks, and I will go into much more detail about how you can do this around your home throughout the book.

East Meets West

When I first started to learn about Feng Shui, I felt quite overwhelmed by how complicated it seemed. It also felt like my house fell short in so many areas that I couldn't physically change. Did we have a door facing south or west? And if it was facing the "wrong" way because it had been built a number of years ago with no Feng Shui principles in mind, what exactly could I do about it? Did we sleep in the "coffin position" facing east? I had no idea if we did or didn't and I didn't know if I could change many of these things even if I wanted to.

Luckily, there's so much more to Feng Shui than simply arranging furniture or adding a few lucky charms. At its core, Feng Shui is about creating harmony between you and your environment whether you rent a room or live in an apartment or a house. The aim is to clear out stagnant, negative energy and make space for positive energy to flow freely throughout your space. When the energy is balanced, it naturally supports your well-being, boosts your mood and creates a sense of ease in your daily life. A well-balanced home feels good. It can help reduce stress, improve focus and even enhance sleep. More than that, the principles of Feng Shui are designed to positively influence key areas of life, from health and relationships to career success and financial abundance. When energy moves freely, opportunities seem to open up, relationships feel smoother and life flows with less resistance.

My goal when working with clients is to help them transform their homes into supportive, nurturing spaces that reflect their personal goals and lifestyles. Modern life can be chaotic, and our homes should be places that recharge us, not drain us. By applying Feng Shui in a modern way, I help people create homes that truly work for them. Whether it's a subtle shift in layout, a mindful decluttering process, or introducing elements that bring warmth and balance, Feng Shui is about making small, intentional changes that create a big impact.

First of all, we need to realize that we are surrounded by energy. We often experience this with people because when we meet somebody whom we like, we instantly feel their good vibrations; and the opposite feeling is true when we dislike someone. We use the saying "They're not on my wavelength", which just means that they aren't on the same energetic vibration as we are. Feng Shui is about understanding the energetic vibration of a space and, for whatever reason, we sometimes forget that buildings have energy – and it can be really powerful. For example, our homes may have absorbed some of this energy from previous owners, so if the past three owners have got divorced while living in your home, maybe there's a residual energy that could be causing arguments. However, some homes – where people are happy and healthy, and opportunities seem to present themselves all the time – have amazing energy. The most obvious time we notice this is when we are looking to purchase or rent a property. As soon as you walk in the door, you get a feeling, good or bad, as to whether or not you feel comfortable in the space, and this is the energy in the home. It's not something you can necessarily put your finger on, but it's such a strong feeling that many of us make one of the biggest financial decisions of our lives based on it.

Energy is also known as Chi (Qi) and in Feng Shui it is often referred to as the life force that flows through your home. Think of it as a gentle breeze flowing through your home, and when it moves freely, life feels balanced and opportunities flow. When it's blocked or stagnant, challenges can arise.

Some homes have great energy and some don't. According to Feng Shui, only about 1 in 40 homes are naturally built in the ideal direction that aligns with the flow of positive energy (or Chi) to attract luck, prosperity and overall well-being. The orientation of a home plays an important role in determining how energy moves through the space, affecting everything from financial success and career growth to health and relationships. You know those people who just have luck in their lives, or they can manifest pretty much anything they like? Well, their home probably has been built in a way that attracts this natural, amazing energy. And for the rest of us who feel like we are wading through mud, our homes most probably aren't aligned like this and are likely to have a lot of stagnant energy blocks that need clearing.

I think Feng Shui is sometimes seen as quite a strict practice because it uses words like "good" and "bad" – for example, a certain alignment is "good for money" or "bad for well-being". But the way I practise Feng Shui means I believe that almost everything can be remedied, and I will be sharing these tips with you in this book

Feng Shui and Mental Well-Being

Have you heard of Taoism? Taoism encourages being in flow with the natural rhythms of life rather than fighting against them. It teaches that when we align ourselves with nature, life feels easier, more balanced, and full of possibility, and this can have a very positive impact on our mental well-being.

One of the biggest Taoist influences in Feng Shui is the concept of Chi, the invisible energy that moves through everything, including our homes. Taoism also advocates creating good Chi within ourselves. You can do this by slowing down, breathing deeply, moving your body gently and giving yourself quiet moments to reflect or meditate. It's also about staying calm, eating well, listening to your gut and living in tune with nature. When we do these things, our energy flows better and life feels easier.

At the core of Taoism is the belief that everything in life is about balance. You may know the terms "Yin and Yang" – these two forces are opposites yet completely interconnected, constantly shifting to create harmony in nature and in our homes. This is something we can actively apply because Feng Shui helps us balance Yin and Yang energy in our living spaces, so that they support rather than drain us. Too much Yin (darkness, stillness, cold, soft textures) can leave a home feeling heavy, dull or even depressing. It's like staying in bed all day – restful at first but draining over time. Too much Yang (brightness, noise, strong colours, sharp lines) on the other hand, can make us feel overwhelmed, restless or hyperactive.

Taoism teaches that when Yin and Yang are unbalanced, we feel it mentally and emotionally. If our lives are too Yang and we are always busy, loud and overstimulated, we might struggle with burnout, stress or anxiety. But if we have too much Yin and lack light, movement or action, we may feel lethargic, unmotivated or even depressed.

A balanced home leads to a balanced mind, and I will be sharing all the ways you can help achieve this in your home throughout this book.

TAOISM PRINCIPLES

- ◆ Letting go of the need to control everything and trusting the process

- ◆ Simplifying life and removing unnecessary stress

- ◆ Moving with change rather than resisting it, like water flowing around obstacles

- ◆ Finding joy in the present moment instead of constantly chasing the next big idea

Feng Shui and Neurodiversity

Feng Shui isn't just about how a space looks but it's also about creating an environment that feels good and supports the well-being of everyone in the household. During my teacher training, I learned firsthand how the right environment can transform a person's ability to focus, feel safe and thrive, especially for neurodiverse students. The same principles apply to our homes; when we design with awareness, we create spaces that support every individual's unique energy and needs. Feng Shui can be beneficial because it gives practical ways to create a space that reduces being overwhelmed and most importantly provides a sense of security. It can be as simple as intentionally arranging furniture, balancing the energy of colours in the home and minimizing sensory distractions, which all help to create a space that feels calm and happy for everyone.

I am honoured to know the incredible Amanda Hawes, a respected expert in educational and developmental psychology. With a master's degree in the field, Amanda has dedicated her career to supporting children, adolescents, young adults and their families. She is passionate about helping neurodiverse individuals find a sense of calm in their lives at home, school, work and within their community.

Amanda's work is truly transformative, focusing on reducing anxiety, managing sensory sensitivities and creating environments that support well-being. She not only provides effective strategies for navigating daily challenges but also empowers individuals by helping them understand how their brain processes the world around them. Amanda's insights and expertise are invaluable, so I asked her professional opinion about how to create a home that supports everyone, and this is what she said.

"Sensory sensitivity can significantly influence how neurodiverse individuals experience and interact with their home environment. For example, individuals with autism or ADHD (attention deficit hyperactivity disorder) may find certain sounds, textures, smells or lighting overwhelming, leading to heightened stress or discomfort. Research suggests that sensory overload can trigger anxiety and reduce the ability to relax or focus (Ashburner et al., 2013). It is therefore important to create a sensory-friendly home by reducing the overwhelming stimuli, such as loud noises, crowded rooms,

strong fragrances or fluorescent lighting, and incorporating calming elements like soft textures and neutral calming colours. When a person enters a sensory-friendly or low-sensory environment, it can create a sense of safety and comfort for many people. Feeling safe and comfortable allows a person to create the essential foundations of positive mental health and overall well-being."

In the coming chapters, I will share more insights from Amanda Hawes on how to create a sensory-friendly home environment, as well as practical tips to support the well-being of everyone in the household.

The Ripple Effect of Feng Shui

There's a beautiful old Chinese proverb that really captures the ripple effect of Feng Shui that starts from within.

"Where there is light in the soul, there is beauty in the person. Where there is beauty in the person, there is harmony in the home. When there is harmony in the home, there is honour in the nation. And when there is honour in the nation, there is peace in the world."

I love this because it highlights something so important: that our surroundings reflect our energy, and vice versa. When we feel good inside, it naturally spills over into our homes, creating a space that feels warm, inviting and full of good energy. And when our homes feel balanced, it has a knock-on effect on our relationships, work and our day-to-day lives. This is the essence of modern Feng Shui – it's not just about arranging furniture but about creating spaces that nurture our souls, strengthen our relationships and ultimately contribute to a more peaceful world.

PART ONE

LET ME INTRODUCE YOU TO FENG SHUI

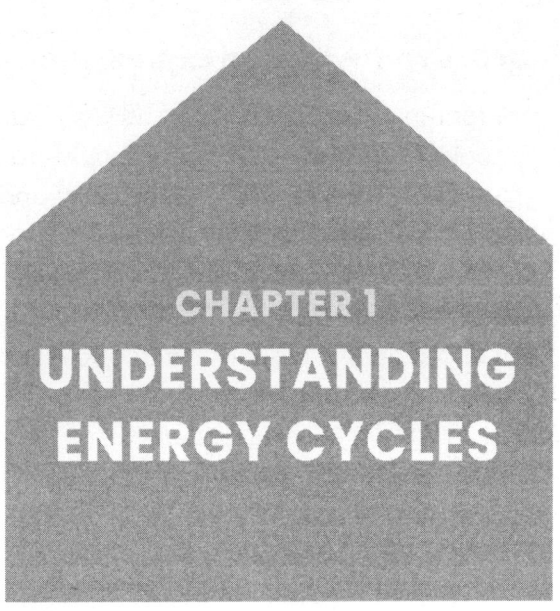

CHAPTER 1

UNDERSTANDING ENERGY CYCLES

Energy never stands still, and in nature it moves in cycles. We have the daily cycle from dusk until dawn and the four seasonal cycles that take us from growth in the spring to rest in the winter. In Feng Shui, there are two other energy cycles: the Nine-Year Cycle and the Twenty-Year Cycle.

The Nine-Year Cycle

According to Feng Shui, the universe moves in cycles of nine years, each bringing a unique energy with it. Some years are great for growth and transformation, while others need patience and stability. Here is a breakdown of what you may have experienced in previous years and what to expect in the coming ones.

2024 – Year 3: Creativity and Expression

This is the year for fun, expansion and creative ventures. It is a particularly social time with lots of opportunities to express yourself. There may also be conflict, competition and arguments.

2025 – Year 2: Growth and Relationships

This is the year of patience, balance and deepening emotional connections. It's the time to focus on connections, friendships and self-care. There is also an illness energy around this year so it's important to look after yourself and concentrate on your own well-being.

2026 – Year 1: New Beginnings

This is the time for a fresh start, so begin to take steps now for the future. It is a great period for new projects, relationships and for setting long-term goals. It's also a good year for career success.

2027 – Year 9: Completion and Transformation

This is the year of letting go of the old to make space for new beginnings. It's time to bring closure to areas of your life that no longer serve you and to concentrate on renewal. It's a very powerful year for manifestation, too.

2028 – Year 8: Power and Abundance

This is the year for success and financial growth. It's also the time when you will be rewarded for all your past efforts, as well as a great year for career and investments.

2029 – Year 7: Reflection and Inner Growth

This is the year for personal discovery, spiritual awakening and deep thinking. It's important to concentrate on communication during this period and just be aware of potential deception.

2030 – Year 6: Love and Home

This is the year to concentrate on family, relationships and nurturing your home environment. It's also a time to make deeper connections. However, remember to stay disciplined and try to avoid distractions.

2031 – Year 5: Change and Adventure

This is the year of change, surprises and breakthroughs. It's a great time for travel, new opportunities and stepping out of your comfort zone. But you may encounter obstacles, so stay focused and be open to change.

2032 – Year 4: Stability and Hard Work

This is the year to lay strong foundations, be disciplined, and think about focusing on long-term security. It's also a wonderful year for love and romance.

The 20-Year Cycle

According to Feng Shui, it is believed that every 20 years there is a major shift in the energy of the world. You can see below the different cycles and that we entered Cycle 9 in 2024. This shift not only affects how we design homes in Feng Shui but also the global trends we see unfolding. Homes built or renovated during different cycles hold different energies, which is why some feel naturally abundant, and others stuck.

Cycle 9 (1844–1863)
Cycle 1 (1864–1883)
Cycle 2 (1884–1903)
Cycle 3 (1904–1923)
Cycle 4 (1924–1943)
Cycle 5 (1944–1963)
Cycle 6 (1964–1983)
Cycle 7 (1984–2003)
Cycle 8 (2004–2023)
Cycle 9 (2024–2043)

The Feng Shui New Year is different to the Lunar New Year because it begins in February. It aligns with the Chinese Solar New Year and February marks the start of spring. For example, Cycle 9 started in February 2024 and will finish in February 2043.

Looking Back to Cycle 8 (2004–2023)

Each Cycle is associated with an element and Cycle 8 is ruled by the Earth, which represents stability, wealth, real estate and long-term planning. It is also associated with mountains and signifies endurance, discipline and spiritual growth.

Historically, Cycle 8 is known for economic booms and real-estate expansion. Between 2004 and 2023 there were huge wealth shifts and digital transformation. The global financial crisis happened in 2008; Bitcoin was created in 2009; between 2010 and 2020 there was a massive rise in real-estate investment; and in 2019–2020 we experienced the COVID-19 pandemic, which led to home-based living, enforced remote working and a vast digital transformation. That was then followed in 2022–2023 by the rise of artificial intelligence (AI) and digital businesses, with remote working becoming ever more popular and widespread.

Cycle 9 (1844–1863 and 2024–2043)

Cycle 9 is ruled by the Fire element, which represents transformation, innovation, visibility and passion. Fire is also associated with fame, technology, spirituality and upheaval, and history shows that Period 9 often brings major shifts in these areas.

The mid-19th century was a time of massive change. The Industrial Revolution was in full swing, introducing exciting new technologies and transforming the way people lived and worked. At the same time, the Gold Rush triggered a surge of economic growth, especially in the USA and Australia. And then came the American Civil War, which was an intense and transformative period that, in many ways, reflected the fiery energy of the era, exposing deep societal truths and forcing change. It was a time of awakening, upheaval and reinvention.

Interestingly, this wave of transformation wasn't just metaphorical, it was quite literal, with devastating fires sweeping through major cities around the world. Some of the most damaging included The Great Pittsburgh Fire (1845, USA), The Great Fire of Toronto (1849, Canada), San Francisco's infamous series of fires (1849–1851) – with the worst in 1851 wiping out 75 per cent of the city, and The Great Newcastle Fire (1854, Australia), one of the most destructive in the country's history. Nonetheless, the UK escaped anything of significance during this period.

These fires were undeniably tragic, but they also cleared the way for rebuilding and renewal, much like the broader societal shifts of the time. While it was a period of great destruction, it was also one of growth, reinvention and new possibilities.

The Period of Change

Cycle 9 is symbolized by the transformative energy of the Rising Phoenix and the illustration above gives you an idea of what it looks like.

The Rising Phoenix is filled with beautiful reds and yellows. It has large wings, and the Phoenix rises through the clouds, basically giving the message, "HERE I AM!" and "Now it's my time to shine".

So, what has that got to do with us? Quite simply it means that we are currently surrounded by an energy that gives us permission to be the person we really want to be.

At the beginning of 2024, we moved from Cycle 8, an Earth cycle that was stable, secure, grounded and strong, to Cycle 9, which is controlled by the Fire element. I'd like you just to take a moment and think about the physical differences between Earth and Fire – they are very different energies.

In nature, fire is something we naturally avoid because it is so destructive. However, the Fire element can be quite beautiful because it has the ability to burn through negative energy. One of its tasks is to cut through all the nonsense in the world and unearth some of the truths that may have been covered up for a while – think about the political and celebrity "news" that is always coming to the surface.

The Fire energy can also light you up and give you positive energy. It's very powerful and it's also great for attracting passion, fame and clients or customers. Therefore, from a commercial point of view, it's a great Cycle in which to start a new business.

As we move from Cycle 8 to Cycle 9, you may have noticed a difference on a personal level. Cycle 8 was dominated by a young, masculine energy of hustle, achievement and external success. During Cycle 8, personal growth was often measured by external achievements such as career success, financial stability and productivity. There were huge trends in goal setting, and discipline and competition were very much welcomed – unfortunately often at the cost of mental health and personal fulfilment.

Cycle 9 represents a mature, feminine energy that is associated with intuition, compassion, creativity, sensitivity, collaboration and connection. Personal growth is shifting from external success to internal fulfilment and people are prioritizing mental health, emotional intelligence and spiritual growth over concentrating solely on financial or career success. The shift from "work hard, play hard" to "work smart, live well" could not be more true because I believe that people now want careers that align with their values, passions and energy.

This is exactly what I felt when I was learning about Feng Shui, and I believe it's where my energy is coming from.

I'm not questioning the ancient art of Feng Shui at all, I'm just blending it with modern living – so it's my way of saying there's another way of doing it. I think this energy literally must have come knocking at my door and said, "Hi Kimberley, welcome to Cycle 9. I's your time to shine."

So, just ask yourself this, do you feel the same way? Do you feel that you've been put in a metaphorical box for so long – maybe for the last 20 years or perhaps even for your whole life – and, all of a sudden, you've got this deep gut feeling that you don't want to do this anymore? You may hanker for a change of career or to live your life differently. You want to speak up. You wish to be the person you really are. You have a desire to speak your truth about things. This is the energy that we are currently surrounded by – and it's so beautiful.

I'm sure you've worked out by now, that Cycle 9 really is the period of change and those who are ready for change will absolutely thrive. For example, that change might take place in the workplace and your current job, or it could be a move to live in a new city or country. And to achieve this, it's more than likely you will need to make changes at home as well.

When we left the UK, I was very much the school mum with a part-time job. I did the majority of the school runs, took my daughter to sporting events and cooked dinner as my husband was out at work for most of the day. Nevertheless, as my business started to grow, our roles within the house began to shift. And now my husband does the school run, knows the school club routine and gets the uniforms ready, and I'm the one who really has no idea what's going on. We've gone through a complete role reversal, which has been amazing, as I would not be able to do what I do without him. And, annoyingly, his dinners are better than mine – not that I would ever tell him that!

The other wonderful thing about the Fire element is that it brings collaboration, because Fire can't burn by itself. It needs all the other elements to burn. That's the cooperative feeling we are experiencing – we are embracing teamwork rather than competition. Fire also brings passion, expansion and aggression. Personally, I really feel that aggression, but not in a bad way. I just feel so driven to spread the magic of Feng Shui around the world to as many people as possible that I will do pretty much whatever it takes to do that. You may be feeling the Fire energy too – to the point where you are almost angry that you've not done something before. If so, you are experiencing what feels like an awakening. You are ready to make leaps and bounds in whatever direction you want to move forward.

Cycle 9 also predicts that there's going to be an even bigger shift in digitalization. There has been a huge rise in AI; classroom education has merged with online learning; and, from a personal point of view, if it wasn't for this shift, I would not be able to do what I do. My Online Business Manager is in the UK, my Branding team are in the UK and South Africa, and my clients are in all corners of the world from Bermuda and New Zealand, to America, France and Australia. I do it all from my home in the Gold Coast, Australia, which I am beyond grateful to be able to do.

Therefore, if you have a business that is customer-facing, think about ways you can make the most of the current strong energy surrounding digitalization and technology. Having a social media account is now as important as having a website, if not more so. Don't get me wrong, starting my Instagram account was one of the scariest things I've ever thought of doing. It wasn't until I started using social media that I realized my face wasn't symmetrical, my hair had thinned and my teeth were wonky and, also, that I tend to wear the same clothes pretty much every day! But that's how I am, and people accept me that way. It was only me who had an issue with the way I looked. I realized that when it comes to social media, you must decide not to let yourself get in the way. I very much see myself as being a messenger for Feng Shui and I had to stop worrying about my image. So please, if you only take one thing from this, make sure you get out of your own way and just let yourself be amazing and successful as you ride the wave of this beautiful energy.

Harnessing the Power of the Rising Phoenix

The Rising Phoenix is a powerful symbol in Feng Shui, representing rebirth, success and resilience. It embodies transformation, helping you overcome challenges and come back stronger than before. You can bring this energy into your home and your life by printing off a picture of a Rising Phoenix from the web, but make sure it's in colour as you want to use the power of the Fire energy. Then write your intentions (see page 38) for the year on the back and place it in the South area of your home as this is linked to visibility and success (chapter 2 will introduce you to the Nine Areas of your Home and I go into much more detail about this there).

Cycle Energy and Health

Every Cycle is linked to specific areas of the body that we need to look after more than usual. Cycle 9 is associated with the heart, eyes, small intestine and lungs. Consequently, we should watch out for issues such as heart disease, high blood pressure, eye strain and emotional burnout. The number of clients who have emailed to say that their eyesight has deteriorated in the last couple of years is quite incredible. This applies to me too and I now have my first pair of glasses, which I am wearing as I write this book. The physical health of our eyes is important, but we also need to be aware of what information we are seeing and bringing into our minds. We weren't built to take in all the data we now consume on social media and on the news 24/7. Start by checking who you follow on social media. Do all the people you're following make you happy? Or do some of them just make you feel inadequate and think, *"How come they've got their lives so together and I absolutely haven't?"* This is your permission to stop following them!

We also need to look after our heart in Cycle 9, and so we must try to get moving. We need to be fit and strong to keep the heart muscle in the best health. The energy also links to "heartache" and how we feel about what we look at on social media, because this can have a big impact on our health. Please be super-aware of what both you and your children are seeing on social media and protect yourselves. What we see and feel influences our mind, too. Remember that you are in charge of what you consume. You don't have to watch the news every day or go on the doom scroll of news, and you don't have to follow situations or people on social media.

When I started my social media journey, I learned about how the algorithms work. Algorithms are little computer robots that work out what we apparently like and don't like on social media, and they do this by calculating how long you read a post or watch a video for. If it's more than three seconds, the robots think you like it so they will send you more of the same. So, train yourself. I know it can be hard because I get sucked in myself – I watch a video and think *"Oh, no, this a really awful story!"* and I'm pulled in. The algorithms then decide I love that sort of stuff and send me more, which just makes me feel low. When something a bit sad (or worse) comes up, make sure you scroll on immediately. If you keep that up, you won't see depressing items anymore and your feed will be filled with a beautiful and perhaps more wide-ranging mix of videos. These days, mine tends to offer funny dog videos, cats tearing up houses and yachts in Italy!

Additionally, Cycle 9 tells us to pay attention to the health of our small intestine, so we need to be very aware of what we feed ourselves. There are more questions than ever currently being asked about what is in the food we eat, and the impact our food has on our overall wellness. This is reflected in the rise of books exploring the impact of ultra-processed foods on both personal health and society. One example is *Ultra-Processed People: The Science Behind Food That Isn't Food* by Dr Chris van Tulleken, which was a Number 1 bestseller on Amazon (Amazon, 2025).

Finally, Cycle 9 is linked to our lungs due to the Fire element associated with it. In the Five Elements Cycle. Fire controls Metal and as Metal governs the lungs and respiratory system, an imbalance of Fire energy (such as excess stress, pollution or inflammation) can impact lung health. Therefore, it is important to be aware of our environment and the air quality we are surrounded by, as well as overall respiratory health, and to incorporate exercise into our daily routine.

In fact, moving helps all the parts of the body and our minds. Personally, I exercise 50 per cent for my physical health and 50 per cent for my mental health. If I don't go for a walk every single day, I know that I am not going to be the best version of myself. Sometimes I listen to a podcast, sometimes I just tune in to my surroundings or walk with a coffee – and, my goodness, do I feel better after the exercise. Give yourself permission to go out there and make time for things that make you feel better. I aim for what I call a

Sustainable Seven on my happiness scale. If you're 10 out of 10, you are elated, bouncing off the ceiling – life could not be better. But being a 10 out of 10 all the time would be exhausting. Believe me, I don't wake up a 7 out of 10 every day but I have a wellness checklist of things that I can do to get me there.

Now, don't feel that you have to go out and run a marathon every single day. I got overtaken the other day while jogging by someone walking. Brilliant! You really don't need to do more than just put one foot in front of another. I promise you that this will make such a difference for reaching a Sustainable Seven. I'd love you to have a little think now and perhaps make a note of ten things that make you happy – just small things that you can do every day, such as walking, listening to music or a podcast, or simply lighting a lovely candle. Then, no matter what number you wake up at, you have the tools you can use to work up to the next number and so on, until you reach the magical Seven.

By tuning into how energy shifts over time, you can make small, intentional adjustments that create big, positive changes in your life and your home. It's about creating a space that feels good now but also one that continues to evolve with you and those who live in your household.

CHAPTER 2

THE NINE AREAS OF THE HOME

In Feng Shui, we divide the home into nine different areas, each representing a different area of our life, a different person in the home and different areas of our body. The table below outlines this.

Compass Direction	Life Area	Person	Body Part
Southeast	Wealth, prosperity, abundance, success and financial growth	Eldest daughter	Liver, hips and thighs
South	Fame, reputation, recognition and self-worth	Middle daughter	Eyes, heart, small intestine, lungs and overall circulation
Southwest	Love and relationships	Mother	Digestive system and abdomen

East	Family and community	Eldest son	Feet, legs, gallbladder
Centre	Health – physical and mental health and overall well-being	Entire household	Stomach, spleen and muscles
West	Children, fertility and new beginnings	Youngest daughter	Lungs, mouth and skin
Northeast	Knowledge, wisdom, personal growth, learning, intuition and spiritual growth	Youngest son	Hands, fingers and back
North	Career, business, life's journey	Middle son	Ears, kidneys, reproductive organs
Northwest	Helpful people and travel	Father	Head, brain and lungs

Locating these Nine Areas in your home is the first place to start with Feng Shui, and I am going to tell you how to do this.

How to Find the Nine Areas of Your Home

The ideal home from a Feng Shui perspective would be a perfect rectangle or square house like a stately home or those homes that look like dolls houses, because this makes it really easy to divide them into nine equal areas.

Start by locating the central area and then from there you can find the rest of the eight areas. If you live in a single-story home or an apartment, you will have one of each of these areas, but if you live in a two-storey dwelling, you will have two central areas; a three-storey home would have three central areas, and so on. If you share a house with others, then you can divide your own room into the nine sections. We don't include the loft or basements in the mapping of the home unless you use these as living spaces – if they are only used for storage, we can ignore them. We also don't include garages or outdoor living areas because Feng Shui concentrates on the energy within the building, as this is what surrounds us the most and therefore has the most impact on us.

Finding these areas can be a really nice way of getting to know our homes because we often overlook the importance of building a relationship with them. Let's face it, they are probably the most expensive thing we ever buy or pay for monthly, and where most of our money goes!

Feng Shui also allows you to look at your home with a fresh pair of eyes because it's amazing how we get used to the items we are surrounded by, and these could be having a huge impact on our lives. I got a message from a lady who had never noticed that the stained-glass window on her front door was actually a picture of a dagger with blood dripping below it! Something like this could have a big impact on the energy of the home and may cause a lot of unnecessary tension or arguments. We just don't really see things we look at every day.

Some homes aren't perfectly square or rectangular and could be missing one or more of the Nine Areas. If your home is missing one of these areas, then the energetic impact of this is that you may find that you are struggling with that area of your life or the person it relates to finds life that little bit harder.

How to Create a Floor Plan

The easiest way to map your home is to use a floor plan (see Figure 1 below). You may have this from when you purchased or rented your home, so have a look online to see

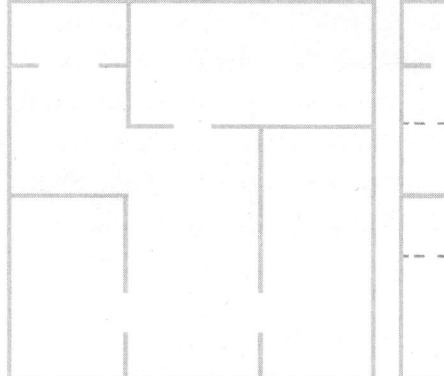

Figure 1. Sample floor plan

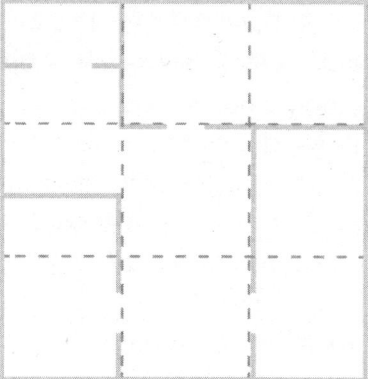

Figure 2. Sample floor plan with 3 x 3 grid lines superimposed

if it is still there. It might be that you have the same floor plan as a neighbour and you can use that; as long as it's the same shape and area, it doesn't matter that it's someone else's home. Or if you can't get hold of an official floor plan, you can draw it yourself either using a free website or by hand. I had to draw ours by hand, so believe me, if I can do it, anyone can do it. You will need some grid or graph paper and it's best to start with the outside of your home. Measure the length by walking one foot in front of another and then make each "foot" the equivalent of one square on the grid paper. That way, you know it's perfectly to scale, which is really important.

Next, you need to divide the length and width into thirds to create a 3 x 3 grid like the image above (see Figure 2 above). If your home is completely square or rectangular then this will fit perfectly on top. We look at the floor plan as a whole and do not pay much attention to walls, so you may find that one area of the grid has more than one room in it.

If your home is an L shape and it has an extension out to the side, such as a conservatory or an extended kitchen, simply extend that area outward (see figures 3 and 4 opposite).

Figure 3. Sample L-shaped home floor plan

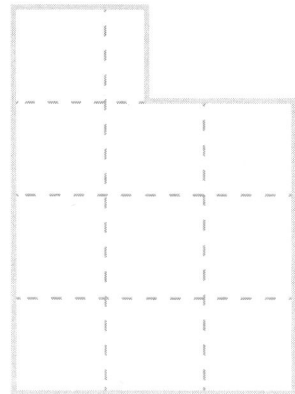

Figure 4. Sample L-shaped home with grid superimposed

It gets a little tricky if the upstairs is smaller or bigger than the ground floor, but the most important floor is the ground because this is where your home is connected to the energy from the Earth. Some homes that are unevenly shaped can be a bit complicated and you may need my help, so I do offer a "Map My Home" service, which is available on my website if you are struggling. At the very least though, you should be able to get a rough idea where the compass points are.

Start off with the Centre point. If your home is an uneven shape, you will still be able to find this by measuring the outside of the main part of the floor plan both horizontally and vertically and finding where they meet in the middle (see Figure 5, page 35).

Once you have found the Centre, stand in this area with the compass app on your phone lying flat in your hand. Take off any jewellery, as this can alter the reading and set it to "true north" in the settings. Or you can use a good old-fashioned hand compass if you like (see Figure 6, page 36).

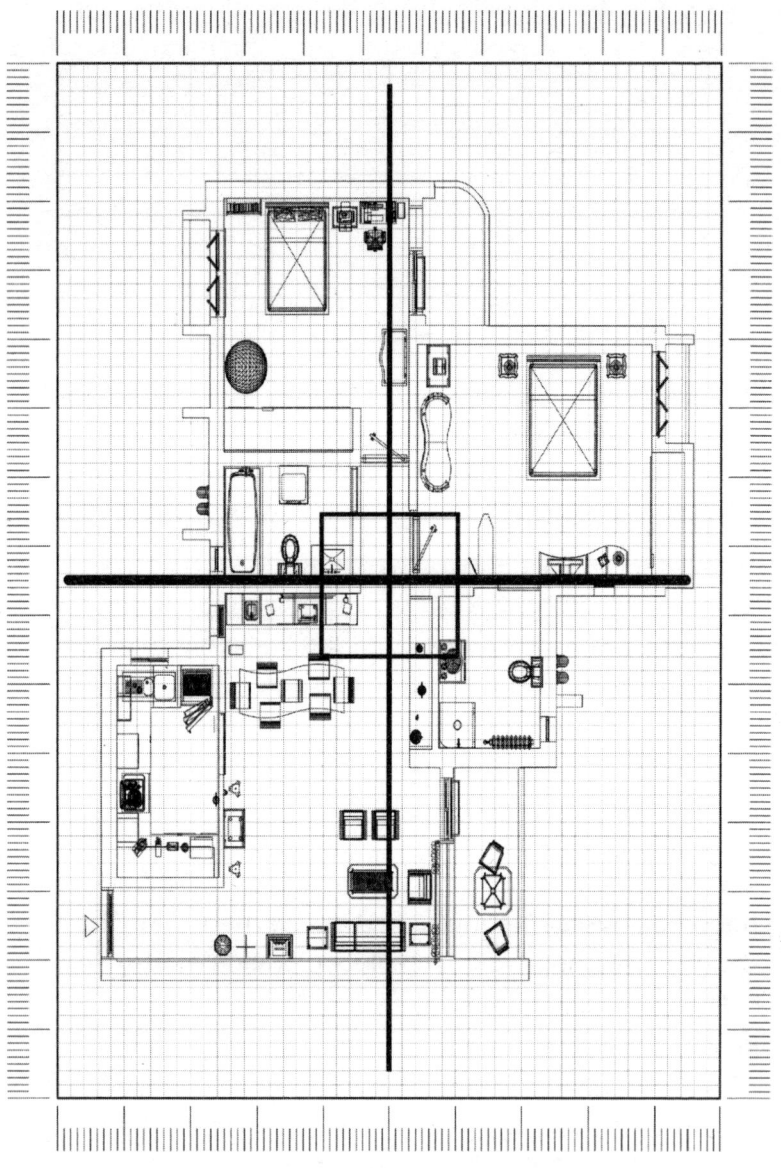

Figure 5.. Finding the centre on an uneven floor plan

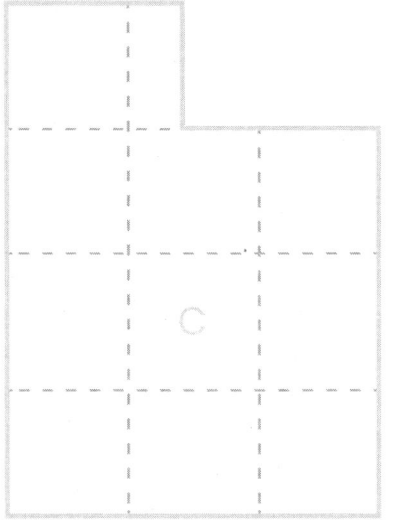

Figure 6. L-shaped sample with the Centre marked on the grid

Now pivot around in a circle until you find North and mark that on the grid along with the other points on the compass. Once you have these you can complete the rest of the areas on the grid. Whichever area the extension comes out from, you simply repeat the same compass directions (see figure 7 below).

And there you have it! You have your own grid of your home. If you don't have the energy to make your own grid, you can guesstimate using your mobile phone. I don't want this process to stop you moving forward through this book and unlocking all the magic your home has to offer.

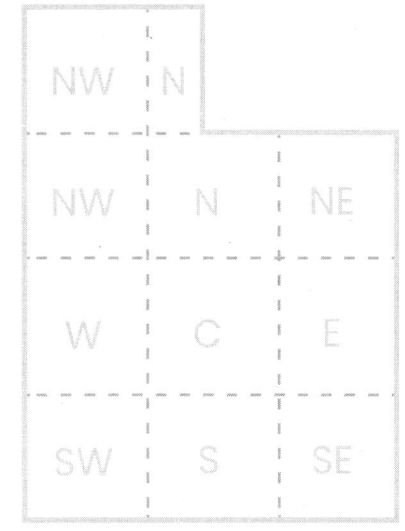

Figure 7. L-shaped sample grid with all the points of the compass filled in

The First Feng Shui Step

Once you have found the Nine Areas and understand what each represents, this will hopefully give you the motivation to declutter these areas, because you will be able to see that perhaps it is your "dumping" room that looks after your health or wealth and all your stuff is causing an energy blockage.

For each of the Nine Areas, I would like you to have a good look around with fresh eyes. What does it look like clutter wise? Is it clean? Do you have anything that is broken in this area? If you have the time, write an inventory (a list of all items) for all the areas, because it's amazing what you can find in the areas that you just forget about.

I know that this is the very unglamorous side of Feng Shui, but it's also important to clean the windows in all areas, because not only does the good energy come in through your front door, but it also comes in through your windows. So, by keeping them clean, the energy will find its way into your home much more easily. Open the curtains in every room as well – even if that means you have to sneak into your teenager's room to do it for them!

It may be that you don't use all the areas in your home, and from an energetic point of view if the door is closed and the drapes or blinds are shut, these areas have almost been put to sleep. I strongly recommend that every day you go into every room in the place, open the door and windows, turn on the lights and "wake up" the room. You could even clap your hands like my mum used to do when she was trying to get me up for school. Come to think of it, she had a little bell at the bottom of the stairs that she used to ring to get my attention! If you are into bell-ringing, you can do this too, but the idea is to make every area of your home awake, alert and working in your favour.

My other tip is to make sure all the areas are as luxurious as possible. I'm not saying that you need to spend a fortune but, for example, adding a soft fluffy towel, nice cushions or hand soaps is really going to help to elevate the energy in these rooms.

For the most important areas of the home, I have dedicated a whole chapter to each (see chapters 5–11) to explain what you can do and what you can avoid, because it really is incredible what can happen just by making the smallest changes.

Setting Your Intentions

Setting intentions in Feng Shui is about aligning your home's energy with your personal goals using the *Nine Areas of your home*. Each area represents a key aspect of life; career, love, health, wealth and more and by making small, intentional adjustments, you can create the right energy to attract what you desire. Whether it's decluttering the North area to invite career opportunities, adding soft, romantic touches in the Southwest for love, or placing symbols of abundance in the Southeast for financial growth, these simple shifts help you focus your intentions and welcome positive change into your life.

I would also like you to write an affirmation for each area that links either to the aspect of life it is associated with or to the person it relates to (see table, pages 30–31), then place it in the relevant area of your home. (I will give you some examples along the way). If you haven't heard of or used affirmations before, all you need to do is write a positive statement about something you want to attract. You should use the present tense, because this helps you to believe that achieving this is possible and it is the shift in energy this belief brings that will help to create change in this area of your life. The most important thing with affirmations, though, is to believe what you are saying. Right from when I started my business, I knew I wanted to be a world-renowned Feng Shui expert. I knew I wanted to write a book and to also have my own television programme. I am aware that as I am writing this down it makes me sound a bit big-headed, but I believed so hard that these things would come true that writing them down didn't faze me. In fact, seeing them on paper just made me more excited. So, for every area of your home, dream big about what you want to attract into your life, because you never know what doors could open for you.

1. The Centre

Let's start with the Central area in your home. You will only have one if you live in an apartment or on a single storey, or more if you live in a multi-storey house. This area looks after health – your physical and mental health, and also self-confidence and anxiety. We start with the Centre as without our health we have nothing. For me, this is the most important area of the home.

There are some small and easy things that you can start doing now in the Central area. As I mentioned earlier, this would be to do an inventory (maybe I need to think of a more fun word for this as it sounds so boring. Let's go with 'homeventory').

You need to do a homeventory of this area and check what you have stored here. Then, remove anything that is broken or chipped as you want the energy to be able to move freely around this area. Unfortunately, "out of sight, out of mind" doesn't work with Feng Shui, so check inside your cupboards and drawers.

I recommend that you don't burn candles in this area, because this burns off the energy of your health and we do not want that. A diffuser is fine, but nothing with a flame.

Then add an affirmation for your Health area. Good examples might be "I am so grateful to be healthy enough to go a walk every day"; "I can move freely without pain and discomfort" or "I play and enjoy sport with my children (or grandchildren)". All family members can get involved with writing affirmations, and you don't have to put them on display – you can tuck them away in a drawer if you prefer.

I also love a visual affirmation around the home. Place a photo here of when you felt amazing or a piece of artwork that shows what you would like to do when you are feeling fit and healthy. I remember that one woman messaged me to say she was really struggling with anxiety, so I asked her what she had in the Central area of her home. From the outside, there wasn't anything in particular that stood out as something that could be impacting the energy surrounding her health, just some ornaments and photos of when she had graduated. I asked her if she had liked university, and her answer was, "It was the most stressful and anxious time of my life"! It sounds so simple, but taking down this photo made a huge difference to how she was feeling.

2. The North

The next area to look at is the North. This relates to your career or business (if you have one) and your life's journey – so it's a pretty important area and a topic I am asked about all the time.

Start with a homeventory. How would you describe this area and does it link to how you feel about your career? Is it cluttered and chaotic? If so, then you may feel that your career is a bit chaotic too, or because the energy can't circulate around this area and gets stuck, you may feel completely lacking in motivation and in a career rut.

I will go into much more detail later in the book (see chapter 13) about jobs and careers and how Feng Shui can help, but here are some tips to help you to start shifting the energy in this area of your home – and therefore in this area of your life.

Write an affirmation such as "I am capable, confident and open to new opportunities" or "Every step I take brings me closer to success and being happy in my career". Dream big and have a wonderful visual affirmation in the North of your home. For example, if your dream is to have a global business, you could have a picture of the world on your wall. I have a print-out of *The Sunday Times* and the *New York Times* best seller logos in my work folder, and I look at them every day, which makes me excited. Doing this is also really motivating for me as I'm sitting here writing my book trying desperately not to get distracted! It's all about raising your vibration – or in other words, getting excited about something! Feng Shui works with our intentions and when I had my home analysed, the intention for me was to have a business that flowed, that was easy and in which I loved my clients – a business that would give me financial independence and allow me to work anywhere in the world. Absolutely everything has come true and I will be forever grateful that I get to do what I do for a living.

3. The Northeast

This area relates to knowledge and skill-building, so it covers all things to do with education, exams, training and personal growth.

It might be that you're training to do something new or that someone else in the house is studying for exams. Or if you or other members of the household struggle with concentration, this is the area in your home to examine. I'm often asked to help people whose children have their final school exams coming up. In these cases, the best thing you can do is to start your homeventory. Then, clear out everything you don't need or no longer use and make it "hotel pristine clean" and as luxurious as possible.

Whoever is studying for exams could write their dream exam results down (which is actually an affirmation) on a piece of paper and place it in this area. Recording the results as if they have happened provokes the excitement, which then hopefully motivates them to do the required studying to achieve the results. And this is why I believe Feng Shui is the missing piece of the manifestation puzzle, because you are writing your affirmations the same way as in the normal manifestation process, but in addition you are clearing the energy in your home and utilizing the specific areas to help. It gives your manifestations superpowers!

The visual affirmation for this area could be of something that you are going to do once you get the exam results. You may be studying toward something specific now, so think about what achieving that qualification will bring into your life. Do your children want to go traveling after their final exams? Do you yearn to find a new job or start a business? Whatever it is, place a picture of what this looks like in this area. It doesn't have to be big; it could just be a greetings card or postcard but enough to get you excited!

4. The East

This area looks after your family and your community. So, this is a really good one if the family dynamics in your home aren't quite as good as you want them to be. Your community can consist of anything from school to your neighbours, or it can include your extended family. Perhaps you would like to attract more friends for yourself and/or your children. If so, this is the area to concentrate on.

As always, start with the homeventory and check specifically for broken or cracked items to dispose of, especially if you feel your relationship with your family or community is tense. This is an excellent area to place family photos, but please only pick photos of family members you like. If you wouldn't invite them round for a cup of tea, they don't deserve a spot on your mantelpiece! It is OK, though, to have photos of family or friends who are no longer with us, and the East is an ideal area to display them. I have a picture of my mum behind me when I work so it's as if she's looking over my shoulder and protecting me. However, I would avoid placing family photos above the fireplace (even it if isn't used) because the burning energy of Fire could be encouraged to burn through your relationship with them, and we absolutely don't want that. A mirror and some candles above the fireplace are perfect items to have here. Photos and pictures of groups of people together having a great time are lovely visual affirmations to have in the home, and for children especially, try placing these types of pictures in their bedrooms as well. You want to encourage a warm and nurturing community feel in your home, where people are welcome, and everyone is loved. Pictures such as snaps of friends having dinner together or having fun on the beach would be a great visual affirmation.

Some examples of good written affirmations for this area are: "My family brings me love, strength and joy", "I am open to making beautiful and meaningful friendships" and "I attract kind, caring people who bring joy into my life".

Children may find the concept of affirmations a little harder, so you may prefer to have conversations with them instead, such as asking them who their "dream friend" might be. Remember that the aim is to raise your or their vibration to attract better or more into your lives, so the way you do this doesn't really matter. You could draw, daydream, talk or write about it – all these actions bring a change to how you feel and that is what we are aiming for.

5. The Southeast

Next is the Southeast area of your home, which looks after your wealth, prosperity and abundance. I'd say this tends to be the second most important area of the home after health. There are also some wonderful and perhaps quirky things that you can do in this area of the home (see chapter 17: Tips for Quick and Easy Fixes).

What is wealth? Well, it can mean something different to everyone. For example, it could simply be money or perhaps a feeling of security. Whatever it is to you, the Southeast of the home looks after this energy. I'm sure you have already guessed, but having clutter and broken items here is going to stop the good energy from being able to flow around, and in some cases, it may stop the energy altogether and create an energy blockage. If you feel like your finances are stuck, or that they are running away quicker than you can earn, this is the place to start. Sometimes, important areas are in what you might consider to be a less-than-ideal room in your home. In the UK our downstairs bathroom and spare room/dump room was in fact in our Southeast. When I found this out, I couldn't have cleaned the spare room quicker if I had tried, but the bathroom is a little trickier because in Feng Shui bathrooms are pretty much classed as "waste rooms". Brilliant! I just had to make the most out of a not-so-great situation and make it as luxurious as possible. I added a soft, fluffy towel, posh soap and hand cream and a little tea light holder with battery candles. And I attempted to keep it "hotel pristine clean".

Once you have made the area as clean, comfortable and gorgeous as you can, it's time to create your affirmations. Something along the lines of "Wealth and prosperity flow easily to me every day" or "I am open to new ways of earning X amount" would do very nicely.

For the visual affirmation, I would choose something that represents wealth to you. Personally, a lucky cat doesn't resonate with me, but it may do with you and if so, that's totally fine. For me, wealth means being able to spend time with my family and go on holiday, so in the Southeast area of our home, I have all our beautiful holiday pictures. They represent wealth because, firstly, they demonstrate that I have the finances to go on holiday and, second, show that I have the time to go away.

I would start with these tasks, but there are many more things you can do in the Southeast and around the home to help improve the wealth energy, which I will reveal later in the book (see chapter 17: Tips for Quick and easy Fixes).

6. The South

This area relates to fame, reputation, recognition and self-worth. Please note that I'm not suggesting you want to be the world's most famous person who does whatever it is that you want to do. It can be as simple as wishing to be recognized for the work that you do, or for being a good parent, a great friend, a lovely sister, brother, aunt or uncle, and so on. Or it can relate to your job. When was the last time someone said thank you to you at work? It's not often we get thanked for what we do. Or it might be that you would love to be known as an expert in your field, or to win an award. The South is the area of your home that looks after all of this. A fresh pair of eyes over the South of your home will tell you if it is helping or hindering this area of your life. Clearing space allows fresh energy to flow through the area, revitalizing this area of your life.

For the affirmations in the South, I am going to ask you to do something a little different (see also page 145). Feng Shui states that the South of the home corresponds to the Fire element and the Rising Phoenix symbolizes this Fire energy, bringing growth and change and helping you to be the person you want to be. The Rising Phoenix is believed to really enhance this change, so I would like you to place a colour picture of the image like the one here in the South area of your home. Then on the back of the picture, write your intention relating to anything you would like

to attract into your life. This might be financial or about your career, relationships, life's journey or anything else that's significant to you. Write it on the back and place this in the South of your home. It doesn't have to be on display – you can hide it if you like and each member of the household can have their own affirmation, if they so choose.

Again, it may be easier to have a conversation with your children than to get them to write down their affirmations. Encourage them to get excited about what they want to achieve, whether it's in sport or academically, or perhaps their ambitions concerning what they want to do when they grow up. Simply allow them to dream. Many sports psychologists believe in the powers of visualization and seeing yourself in your mind's eye winning a race before an event, so teaching them this skill from an early age is a great thing to do.

7. The Southwest

This area in the home represents love, relationships and marriage; therefore, if you wish to attract more love or a new love interest, this is the area you need to concentrate on.

This is a huge topic, and your bedroom can play a key role in enhancing this area of your life. To explore this further, I've dedicated an entire chapter to it (see chapter 11: Restful and Romantic Bedrooms), where I dive into the numerous ways you can transform your bedroom space. As you have already seen (see page 4), this is the topic that first got me interested in Feng Shui, but more because I did not believe for one second that changing things in your home could actually help to attract a partner into your life. How wrong was I?!

8. The West

The West area of your home relates to fertility, children and new beginnings. If you were looking to start a family or have more children, this is where you would focus. Before we moved to Australia, this area was really important to me because it related to new beginnings, so it really is a broad area created from an energy of "newness in your world". Because of this newness, make sure that you don't have anything "old" in this area, such as antiques or decorative clocks that don't work, as this gives off an energy of time standing still.

Fertility is a complex and delicate topic, and I am by no means an expert. Nevertheless, I do believe that you can make improvements to the area in your home that looks after fertility. For example, instead of displaying photos of couples, place artwork or images featuring multiple children to symbolically attract joyful, fertile energy into your life. You can also add a written affirmation here to reinforce your intention, such as: "Our family is growing with love and ease", "I welcome new life into our home with an open heart" or "Our home is filled with joy, laughter and the promise of new beginnings." If you would like to learn more about this, you can listen to a podcast I recorded (Episode 12 of The Feng Shui Flow podcast).

For new beginnings, I frequently use the following affirmation: "Every day is a fresh start filled with endless possibilities", and I really believe this to be true. It excites me that you never know what could happen. You might also like to place a plant in the West of your home to welcome growth energy into this area of your life.

If you are looking to move house, which is also part of new beginnings, place a photo of your dream house or location in the West area. While we were in the planning stages of moving, I had a picture of Bondi Beach as my screensaver, as this motivated me when I was working. Surround yourself with whatever raises your vibrations.

9. The Northwest

Finally, we come to the Northwest area that relates to helpful people and travel. You know those times in life when you just think *"All I want is for somebody to help me with this"* or you feel completely unsupported in certain aspects in your life? For example, you need to find a reliable babysitter/cleaner/virtual assistant/solicitor, etc? Well, this is the area that governs that energy. It also looks after the energy that will help you travel more, and perhaps these seem like very different energies but both require things to "go your way".

This is the final space to do a homeventory – I can hear your sigh of relief from here! Is it cluttered? Do you have a broken suitcase hiding under a bed? I know this is a specific example, but that's exactly what we recently discovered. Patrick has been saying for ages that we could simply replace the wheel rather than buy a new suitcase but, quite frankly, I don't want that bad energy in the house. So, as we speak, a poor, lonely, broken suitcase is sitting next to our bins while we wait for a new wheel to come!

An effective written affirmation for the Northwest could go something like this: "I am surrounded by helpful, kind and supportive people to attract help for particular aspects of my life. And for travel, "I am excited for the new adventures that await me", would be great. You don't have to use these exact words, and for travel, a visual affirmation of wherever you would like to travel is absolutely perfect for this area.

Linking the Areas to People

You can see in the table on pages 30-31 that each of the Nine Areas also links to different people in the household, and you can use this information to help those individuals. It is a bit like putting pieces of a puzzle together, so let me give you an example. Susan was in her 50s (I have changed all names in the book for anonymity) and she suffered terribly with migraines. This information allowed me to associate two areas of the house with her issues. The first step is to link the area to the person, which was the Southwest as this is classed as the mother, and then I looked at the area the issues linked to and that is the Northwest because this looks after the head and brain. I then asked Susan to check both areas for anything that was broken, cracked or not working and to have a good declutter, specifically in these areas. In the Northwest she had a mirror that was cracked and stored in a cupboard, along with loads of other random items. She got rid of the mirror and sorted through the cupboard, getting rid of old items. She then added some great storage solutions, so it was neat and tidy. And guess what? Her migraines reduced significantly. Feng Shui never ceases to amaze me!

There are a couple of things I'd like to point out. If you have only one son, his energy is generally represented by the Eldest Son in Feng Shui, which corresponds to the Family area, located in the East. However, depending on his age and life stage, his energy could also connect with the Middle Son area (Career and Life Path – North) if he is in his teens or early adult years and focused on personal growth or his career. Or it could be connected to the Youngest Son area (Knowledge and Wisdom – Northeast) if he is still young and in a stage of learning and development.

If you have only one daughter, her energy in Feng Shui is generally associated with the Youngest Daughter, which corresponds to the children and new beginnings area in the West. Nonetheless, depending on her age and life stage, she may also resonate with the Eldest Daughter area (Wealth and Abundance – Southeast), particularly if she is independent, career-driven and/or taking on a leadership role in the family. If she is in a phase of developing relationships and personal connection or already married, she may connect well with the Mother area (Love and Relationships – Southwest).

So, there you have it. We have covered the first in-depth layer of Feng Shui, and once you have identified these areas in your home, you can start to uncover Feng Shui's magic and welcome in all the wonderful opportunities that are waiting for you. I'm excited for you!

Intention Activation Checklist

☑ 1. **Declutter:** Clear stagnant energy to make space for new opportunities

☑ 2. **Write It Down:** Place a written affirmation in the corresponding area

☑ 3. **Visualize It:** Spend a moment each day imagining your intention coming to fruition

☑ 4. **Add Visual Affirmations:** Place objects, photos or pictures that represent your goal in the corresponding area

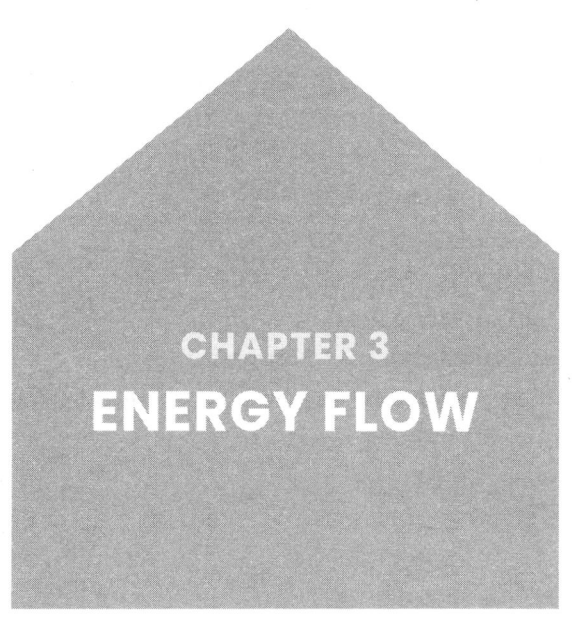

CHAPTER 3
ENERGY FLOW

Our home isn't just a collection of walls and furniture, it's a living, breathing space that affects how we feel every day. Think of Chi (energy) like air or water, constantly moving and shaping our mood, health and overall vibe. When the energy is flowing well, everything feels light, fresh and uplifting, as if your home is giving you a big, supportive hug. But when energy gets stuck or sluggish, you might notice that you procrastinate more, that you have low energy or perhaps lack motivation. And then there's negative Chi – the kind that feels sharp, overwhelming or just a little off – and it's often caused by clutter or sharp objects in the home because the energy simply cannot move freely around the home.

Energy enters the home primarily through the front door (in an apartment, the energy will enter via your balcony or windows that have a view, rather than your entrance door).

This is often called the Mouth of Chi in Feng Shui, and it is where the good energy flows in and sets the mood for the whole space. If your entrance is open and welcoming, then fresh opportunities and positive energy can easily enter. If it's blocked, cluttered or neglected, the energy struggles to flow, and you might feel stuck or uninspired. Amanda Hawes has an amazing idea for cluttered hallways and that is to create a "landing pad" for each household member, where each person has a designated zone to keep their bag, keys, wallet, and anything else they need for the day, and to charge their phone. The creation of a landing pad allows a person to know exactly where their belongings are and saves time looking and searching for them as they are kept all together. This works equally well for neurodiverse and neurotypical individuals.

Beyond the front door, energy also enters through windows, which act like the "eyes" of the home, bringing in light, fresh air and new perspectives. Windows that are dirty, stuck or covered in heavy drapes can dim the energy, while clean, well-maintained ones allow energy to circulate freely.

Even the hallways and pathways inside your home play a role, as they act like roads for the energy, guiding Chi to different areas. If they're open and clear, energy moves smoothly. If they're cluttered or cramped, the flow is disrupted, which can manifest as obstacles in different areas of life. Energy moves along the path of least resistance; the straighter the line, the quicker it moves. And we don't want that, we want the energy to flow slowly around us so that it can nourish all the corners of our living spaces. Homes that have a direct line from the entrance through to the back door are sometimes referred to as "shot-gun" homes because the energy shoots straight in and out without spending any time in the building. Our home has this and it's really easy to fix —

all you need to do is add things to your hallway to help slow down the energy. This isn't an excuse to add loads of clutter though – we are aiming for a mindful décor! Add a side table if you can, or mirrors along the hallway (not opposite the front door though, because this will just bounce the good energy right back out again), and a chandelier-type light fitting or even some crystals to help slow down the energy.

Open-plan homes are fantastic for creating a sense of space, light and connection, but in Feng Shui, the challenge is that energy moves freely in these spaces, which can be a good thing but sometimes also detrimental. For example, if the flow is too strong, you may feel overwhelmed when you are in this space, or if it's too weak, it can create stagnation and may make you feel tense or argumentative and lacking in motivation. Open-plan areas may make it harder for people to relax too, and Amanda Hawes suggests that we try to incorporate quiet zones and low sensory areas, especially for neurodivergent family members. One way of doing this is to try to define each of the rooms so that there are distinct zones for each of the different ways you use the space (for example, in the dining room, living room and kitchen), which helps to slow down the energy and bring a feeling of calm rather than chaos. You can do this with sofas in the living area to make it feel more enclosed, and placing a rug under the dining table will both define and ground the space. You can also try varying the lighting or colours in the different areas. In addition, you can slow down the flow of energy with plants placed in the corners, as well as using soft furnishings like cushions, rugs and throws to help absorb the energy.

Decluttering

Decluttering is a huge part of Feng Shui and, believe me, it's not my favourite task either! However, it's probably a conversation that I have with 99.9 per cent of my clients. When I ask them about the last time they decluttered their home, the most common response is "I know I've got to do it, but I don't have time". This is also a topic that Amanda Hawes has mentioned numerous times.

"Neurodiverse individuals often face challenges such as sensory overload, lack of structure and difficulty with transitions or changing between tasks or activities within the home environment. Sensory sensitivities to noise, clutter, smells or lighting can create significant stress for many people who are neurodivergent. Unorganized spaces or large amounts of clutter may in fact increase their difficulties with executive functioning, particularly for individuals with ADHD (attention deficit hyperactivity disorder) or autism. Executive functions are our necessary cognitive skills that help us plan, focus our attention on a task, remember instructions and manage multiple tasks successfully. Clutter and disorganization have been clinically identified to increase levels of distress and Cortisol, specifically for those with neurodiversity (Saxbe and Repetti, 2010)."

From a Feng Shui point of view, there are two reasons why decluttering is so important. The first is that the good energy needs to be able to move around the home and the more stuff that is in the way, the harder it is for the energy to access all the corners of the home. As the good energy enters our home through the front door, it needs to have room to enter properly. The more shoes, coats and bags that are in the way, the harder it is for that energy to come in and make its way around the home.

When things are in the way, the energy can get stuck and it sits and stagnates. The result is that we may feel stagnant in our lives, as if we have no clear direction. Or we want to move forward, but nothing seems to be going our way. This can then make us feel frustrated, angry, tense and even anxious.

The second reason why we need to declutter is that we may have hung on to items in the home that are holding us back or that don't bring joy and happiness in our lives. It may be items from when your children were little, clothes you no longer fit into, things from previous jobs or even pictures of family members you don't even like, but which have somehow made their way into your home because you feel "bad" for not keeping them or having them on display. So, that's my first tip. Don't feel that you need to keep gifts that you don't like. Secondly, don't put up photos of family members or friends you don't get on with. Every time you walk past them, these items have a negative impact on your energy. As home costs a lot of money to live in, you deserve to feel happy in it!

It's not uncommon to have cupboards, drawers and even rooms full of clutter – and I was just as guilty of this. Before Feng Shui came into my life, our entire spare room was filled with suitcases, ironing, clothes that I promised myself I would take to the thrift store, old toys – the list goes on. The only time I would tidy it up was when people came to stay. That was until I discovered that this room was in fact in the Southeast area of my home, which looked after our wealth, prosperity and abundance (see Chapter 2: The Nine Areas of the Home). Needless to say, I couldn't tidy the room quickly enough! I have heard a thousand different excuses for why people have so much clutter in their home, and I get it. Some people find it really easy to declutter and the process is as simple as "Do I use that?" No – it goes; yes – it stays. But rarely is it that simple because, for many, there's a great emotional attachment to items. I'm actually in the middle –

with some things I'm very black and white. "No, I haven't used that for ages. It's going". And then there are some random things that I keep, like my boarding pass from my first trip back to the UK from Australia for work, because it has an emotional attachment to it and I am super proud that I was able to do that. So, I just want to say that it's OK to keep that kind of stuff.

Having an emotional attachment to items is real, and the thought of not having them can be really upsetting. My mum passed away about 15 years ago now. She had early-onset Alzheimer's and died when she was just 60. She was ALL fun and the friendliest and nicest person you could ever meet – she would love that I'm a Feng Shui consultant now, especially the fact that I've been on TV! Toward the end of her life, she moved into a care home, and perhaps that made it easier to get rid of anything that she didn't take with her. A lot of it was just clothes, so we sent those to the thrift store, and then we kept the more meaningful items like her jewellery. But I did hold on to two items that really make me smile. And that's really important: keeping the things that deep down make you smile. Of all her possessions, I kept her slippers because they're these leopard print slip-ons that, if you knew my mum, literally summed her up. The other item I kept was a fleece. Because sometimes, if I want a cuddle, I can put on that fleece and it's just lovely. They probably didn't mean anything to my mum, and I know they sound like mad things to keep, but they are the items that really remind me of her and they make me happy.

The point is that it's OK to keep stuff that you are emotionally attached to but only if this makes you happy. If I had held on to stuff that reminded me of her being poorly, then that would make me sad every time I thought of her. Whereas every time I open the drawer and see these leopard-print slippers, they really make me smile. So please don't think that I'm an awful, cold-hearted person who comes into your home and gets rid of everything – I'm really not!

I do understand that children's items are often things that people want to hold on to, but do you really need to keep the junk models they made at school? Let's just say that many of my daughter's milk-bottle skyscrapers quickly made their way into the recycling bin!

I have worked with a lot of clients who like to keep their children's paintings around and I'm not going to tell you to get rid of them, but there are other ways of keeping them. For example, you can take photos of artwork and milk-bottle skyscrapers and add them to a photo book. Then, the photo book can live nicely on a bookshelf, and you still have those lovely memories. You are far more likely to flick through a photo book, than you are to go through a box that's been hanging around in your attic for 15 years. You can also buy digital frames that allow you to rotate the photos inside them, which is a really lovely idea as you can then still display them but in a nice way.

One client, whose children were ten and eight, had kept a lot of her children's clothing and toys, as well as their pram – even though she wasn't planning on having another child. This is a great example of keeping things because they hold an emotional attachment, but also because they cost a lot of money, so there was a financial consideration to overcome as well. It was all stored in a room with the door closed, so she didn't have to think about it – very much "out of sight, out of mind". Nevertheless, that just made it a pretty expensive storage room! If you think about price per square footage, how much are you paying to store such stuff in your home?

Hands up if you are the person who has bags of clothes "ready" to sell online. This was me! I had decided that they were too expensive to take to a thrift store, and I had three bags of clothes ready to sell, but it was so complicated with QR codes and leaving bags out on the road for a company to collect, that they sat there for three months. In the end, I just took the bags to the thrift store, which I should have done from the start. If you have the motivation to sell your clothes online, that's amazing – I wish I did! Whether you donate them to a thrift store or sell them on an online second-hand site, these are far better options than keeping items you never use. You're giving somebody else the opportunity to have things that perhaps they wouldn't be able to afford brand new and you are giving the items a new life. For example, with a pram, you're helping new parents who may be unable to afford one like you have because, let's face it, prams are expensive. It's also really good to know that an item is going to be enjoyed and used as it should be, rather than sitting unused in your home.

If you are having a decluttering wobble and you feel guilty or possibly uncomfortable keeping something but are equally reluctant to let it go, you could adopt a two-stage decluttering process. Bag the items up and put them in the garage or the boot of your car and, if after a month you've not thought about them and feel you want to go ahead and get rid of them, take them to the thrift store. But promise me to only hang on to them for one month at the most – please don't keep the bags in your car for months on end!

Here are the areas and items I would concentrate on first.

The Entrance or Hallway

To allow the good energy to enter the home, this space needs to be kept as clear as possible. Try to limit the number of shoes in this area to the ones you use daily, and use something like a box or a basket with a lid on to store them so that the energy is contained inside and isn't seeping into your home. The ideal place to store coats and jackets would be on coat hooks on the back of another door in the house – for example, the toilet – rather than hanging them on the front door. Finally, have a designated spot to store keys and mail to avoid clutter build-up. Each person in the home could have their own little box to put these and other small belongings in.

Your Wardrobe and Shoes

Decluttering your wardrobe in Feng Shui is about so much more than having a tidy space; it's about clearing out old energy and making space for new opportunities, confidence and personal growth. Everything in your wardrobe carries energy from the past, whether that's memories, emotions or even your mindset when you bought the item. If your wardrobe is overflowing, messy or filled with things you don't love, it can contribute to mental fog, stress and indecision.

We beat ourselves up by keeping clothes that we wore a year ago, two years ago, pre-lockdown, pre-kids. And guess what? Our bodies change as we get older and that is completely normal, yet we hold on to these clothes, thinking *"One day I'll fit into them again"*. Or you hang on to them because they cost you a lot of money, you've never worn them or they still have the tags on them.

When we moved to Australia, we literally moved with two suitcases each. At the time this terrified me, but it meant that I only brought clothes with me that gave me joy and happiness. My scruffy clothes didn't make the cut, nor did the comfy but tatty old knickers I'd had for years or the shoes that hurt so much I could only wear them if we were going out for dinner because I couldn't walk in them. I love that I adore every item in my wardrobe now. Keeping clothes that no longer fit, are worn out or remind you of a time you've moved on from can hold you back energetically. Letting go of them creates space for a fresh start and new possibilities. Your clothes represent who you are and how you show up in the world. Holding on to things that don't align with your current self (or your future goals) can create stagnation. By keeping the clothes that make you feel good, empowered and aligned with your best self, you will raise your energy and therefore attract more positive experiences.

As I have mentioned, in Feng Shui letting go of old items makes space for new energy to flow into your life, whether that's new opportunities, personal growth or even new relationships. If you're feeling stuck in any area of life, decluttering your wardrobe can be a powerful way to shift energy. If you are really struggling, you could work with an online stylist. They can tell you what colours suit you and what body shape you are, so you know what items look good on you. Most offer a wardrobe decluttering service to help you decide on what to keep and what to let go of.

Next comes shoes. When was the last time you really went through your shoes? I know that shoes are very expensive. I don't know how it's happened, but I'm sure they have tripled in price over the years! So, I understand why you may want to keep them. But I've also found that shoes go in and out of fashion really quickly. Go through your shoes and make sure you keep only the ones that you wear, and whatever you do, don't store them under your bed because this energy will be making its way up through the mattress and impacting your sleep. Ideally, you wouldn't store anything under your bed because you want the energy to be able to fully circulate around you when you sleep. However, I know that storage is tight in many homes, so if you do have to store something under your bed, go for soft items like towels, bedding, jumpers and so on, and not toys, handbags and shoes. I had one client who came to me because her daughter really struggled to sleep, and it turned out that they stored all their ski equipment under her bed. If you think about it, ski equipment is pointy, sharp and heavy, and this energy was coming up from under the bed. Needless to say, her daughter slept a lot better when they moved these items to another area of the home.

After you have tackled your wardrobe and shoes, we can get down to the nitty-gritty in the house.

Hidden Clutter

The bookshelf was an area in our house that just grew by itself, and nobody really took care of it. It's an awful place for gathering dust and cobwebs and it might be responsible for holding you back in life or for your lack of motivation. This is because if you don't use the books on a regular basis, the energy may become stagnant around the space. Have a look at what books you are keeping there. For example, they may relate to previous jobs or include old diet books, that are no longer relevant to your current life stage. We had about ten books on bird watching – I don't even know where these came from! So have a really good clear-out of your bookshelf.

Cupboards, cabinets and drawers are also important to go through. I most certainly had an addiction to buying kitchen gadgets, from the juicer (which was enormous) and two different types of blenders, to a spiralizer and three different pancake pans. I even kept items that were broken, thinking that one day, they would magically mend themselves. The kitchen can gather clutter without us even realizing it, so keep an eye on the countertops and clear any unnecessary items from there, but don't just dump items in cupboards, cabinets and drawers instead. Also, periodically go through the pantry/larder/kitchen cupboards to discard expired food and organize the space so you know where everything is.

Children's Toys

Children's toys can take up a ridiculous amount of space in the home. It's quite incredible really. I worked with a lady who sent through photos of her home, and it was filled with children's toys. When I asked her about them, she said that her daughter didn't really play with them. I think sometimes if you give children too much choice, they don't really play with anything – I definitely experienced this with my daughter when I had all the toys out. What you could do is have a good clear-up and then almost drip-feed a few toys every week, as quite often they will then play with them more. I think it makes us feel better, seeing a room full of toys because perhaps we didn't have that ourselves, as children. I remember driving my jumbo jet around the house when I was a child and having the time of my life, but looking back it was just a cardboard box and a vivid imagination!

Attics and Lofts

What do you store in your attic or loft? It's often where we put stuff that we don't want to get rid of. Many clients have super-tidy houses and then their attic is absolute bedlam. There are some items that are perfectly OK to store in the attic – for example, Christmas decorations and things that are seasonal, like your clothes. A lady messaged me the other day saying she kept hold of receipts, little ticket stubs and things like that and wondered if she should keep them. Before we moved, I went through our attic and I had kept things from when I first met my husband, such as tickets and flyers, and I got rid of them all. Let's face it, if anything happened to me, my daughter isn't going to want to keep them, and I don't want her to feel guilty about throwing them away. Also, I have the memories of being in New York or wherever we went. I don't need my boarding pass from 1993 to remind me where I went on vacation. If you are looking to move forward with your life, it can be items like these that are holding you back energetically. And if you are sleeping beneath all of these items, you can just imagine the stagnant energy that is seeping down through the ceiling from them. Feng Shui is all about life, energy and growth, so bear that in mind when you begin the decluttering process.

The Garage

The garage is another place to go through and have a good clear-out. Even though it may not be a main living area, your garage still holds energy that influences your entire home. If it's packed with old junk, broken items or things you "might use one day", it can create stagnant energy, making the whole house feel heavy or unbalanced. Things that can be stored in the garage include cars (obviously), car maintenance items, bikes/scooters, tools, gardening equipment, holiday decorations and travel items. Use it as an intentional space rather than a dumping area for unused items. This is especially important if your garage is integrated into the home because any stagnant energy there will be able to enter the home easily.

More about Decluttering

When you declutter, there is no doubt your home will feel lighter. However, I totally understand that it can be a really overwhelming process, too. I don't expect you to be able to do your whole space in one go – do it room by room. To give yourself that extra bit of motivation, go back to chapter 2: The

Nine Areas of the Home because if there's an area of your life that you're struggling with or you believe could be better, that's the perfect place to start. For example, your wealth, prosperity and abundance is governed by the Southeast area of your home, so if you are struggling or think you could improve that area, I would most definitely begin there.

Remember, if you get stuck, ask yourself this: if I move home, would I take it with me? And if the answer is no, then it's time to give the item a new home.

Somebody told me the other day something that I found quite profound, so are you ready? She said that when we buy things, we're only borrowing them for a certain amount of time and what we're paying for is to have them in our presence for a time because we "can't take them with us". So, your house, your clothes, the toys, the computers, the phones – you're really only borrowing them all. If you get into the mindset that you're only borrowing things and you can pass them on for somebody to do the same, it will help you think differently about some of the things in your home. I understand that decluttering is an emotional process. However, the benefits far outweigh keeping a pram or children's artwork for ten years.

See page 205 for the Declutter Checklist that you can use to make sure that every area of your home is covered.

So that's decluttering in a nutshell. I'm not so cold-hearted that I'm going to ask, "Why on earth would you keep that?" After all, I still have my mum's leopard-print slippers.

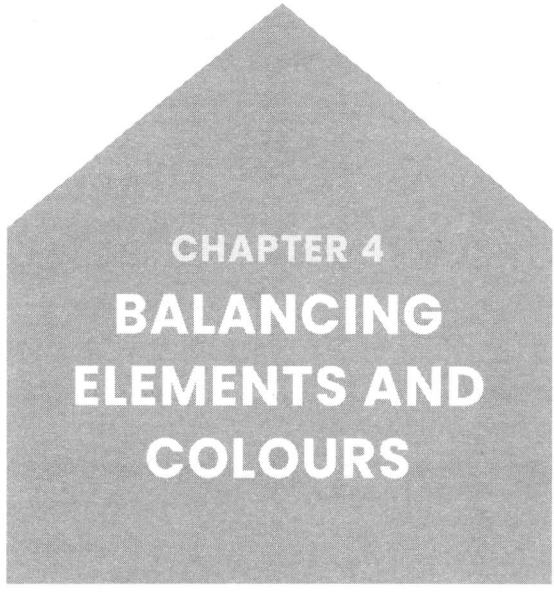

CHAPTER 4

BALANCING ELEMENTS AND COLOURS

In Feng Shui, each of the Five Elements of Wood, Fire, Earth, Metal and Water corresponds to a colour. To create a harmonious space, it's important to balance these elements rather than letting one dominate or weaken another. In nature, the Five Element Cycle does exactly that – it's nature's way of keeping everything in harmony, and I will go into more detail about this below. Each element has a unique relationship with the others, either supporting or controlling them. There are two cycles: one where they help each other to thrive – the Productive Cycle – and the other where they keep each other in check – the Controlling Cycle.

The Productive Cycle

This is the "growth" cycle in which each element nourishes the next, keeping energy flowing smoothly (see figure 8 on the following page):

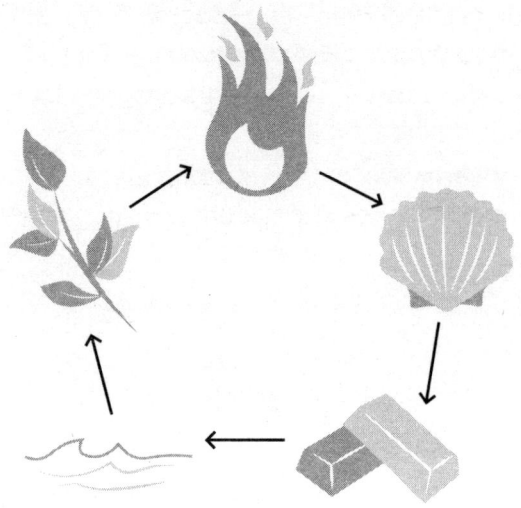

Figure 8. The Productive Cycle

- **Wood feeds Fire** (like logs fueling a flame).
- **Fire creates Earth** (ashes become soil).
- **Earth produces Metal** (minerals and ores form underground).
- **Metal gathers Water** (like condensation on a cold surface).
- **Water nourishes Wood** (helping plants grow).

When these elements are in harmony, a space feels balanced, energized and naturally supportive.

The Controlling Cycle

Just as too much of anything can be overwhelming, the elements also maintain a balancing act in which one keeps another in check, preventing it from dominating the others (see figure 9).

◆ **Fire melts Metal** (think of a blacksmith shaping tools).
◆ **Metal cuts Wood** (axes chopping trees).
◆ **Wood breaks through Earth** (tree roots growing through the soil).
◆ **Earth absorbs Water** (soil soaking up rain).
◆ **Water extinguishes Fire** (pouring water on flames).

Figure 9. The Controlling Cycle

This cycle ensures that no single element overpowers the space, preventing an excess of one kind of energy that could make things feel out of kilter.

By understanding these relationships, you can adjust the energy in your home to suit your needs, whether you want to bring in more vitality, create a sense of calm or simply improve the overall flow.

Using Colour

The key is to use colour intentionally so that energy flows smoothly and supports your well-being. In Feng Shui, colours are more than just design choices – they carry specific energies that influence the mood and the overall harmony of a space, and therefore our well-being. Each colour is connected to one of the Five Elements and can either enhance or balance the energy in a room.

Fiery Colours

The Fire element is all about passion, energy and making a bold statement. Red is the strongest Fire colour and it radiates confidence, vitality and power. It's fantastic for areas where you want to boost energy, like your front entrance or a workspace, but not so great for the bedroom because it's really hard to relax around lots of red. On the other hand, orange brings a lovely social energy that boosts creativity, enthusiasm and connection to an area, making it perfect for living rooms or workspaces where you want an uplifting, dynamic feel. If you're looking for a softer Fire energy, pink is a great choice. It's linked to love, kindness and romance, so it's ideal for the bedroom or the Southwest area of your home, which is connected to love, romance and relationships. Then there's purple, a deeply spiritual colour that promotes wisdom, but be warned, using it in the bedroom might lead to sexual frustration (and nobody wants that!).

While Fire energy is powerful, too much of it can be overwhelming, leading to anxiety, burnout or even irritability. If a space feels too intense or overstimulating, you can cool things down by introducing Water elements like deep blues and blacks or balancing it with Earth tones like creams and beiges to restore a sense of calm and stability.

Woody Colours

The Wood element (think plants and trees) brings a lovely feeling of growth, vitality and health, which can be represented using green and teal shades. Green symbolizes growth, renewal, healing and fresh beginnings, so it's a good choice for bedrooms, offices or any space that you want to "calm down". Sage green would be my suggestion for all these rooms because it's calm but has enough energy to make a difference to the area. Yet too much of the Wood colours in the home can cause restlessness, feeling overwhelmed and the sense that life is all over the place – like you are running round in circles but not actually getting anywhere. To help balance this, you can add Metal tones such as white and grey, which will help to bring more structure, and then some Earth tones like beiges and creams to help ground the energy.

Earthy Colours

The Earth element brings a feeling of stability, grounding and that warm, nurturing energy that makes a house feel like a home. Think of the colours of sand and shells – for example, a soft beige. These nature-inspired colours create a sense of comfort and

security, making them perfect for living rooms, bedrooms and communal areas like kitchens or offices where a steady, balanced feeling is needed. As lovely as Earth energy is, too much of it can leave a space feeling stagnant and uninspiring, almost as if you're stuck in a rut with no motivation to move forward. If your room feels a little too heavy or lifeless, you can add a touch of green or teal (Wood element) to add a bit of energy or perhaps hints of blue or black (Water element) to help create movement and flow to introduce a sense of adaptability. Then you can go with the flow of life and welcome in new opportunities and possibilities.

Metallic Colours

The Metal element brings a feeling of clarity, focus and precision. White is the ultimate "fresh start" colour, bringing in a sense of openness and mental clarity. Grey is a cool and sophisticated neutral colour that can help to balance emotions and it encourages deep thinking, perfect for offices or study spaces where you need to focus. Gold, silver and copper don't just look beautiful, they also amplify abundance and precision, making them great for adding a little prosperity boost. You can do this by simply adding metallic décor, such as picture frames or stylish fixtures.

Used in the right way, Metal colours can help bring structure, calm and a sense of purpose to your home. However, too much of the Metal element can make a space feel cold, rigid and a little too clinical – as if you're living in a showroom instead of a home! You might start feeling overly critical or emotionally distant, or people may appear too stuck in their ways. If this is the case, you can soften this by introducing some Fire energy with warm reds and oranges or grounding Earth tones like creams and beiges to bring warmth, cosiness and a more welcoming vibe.

Water Colours

The Water element is all about flow, wisdom and calmness, making its colours perfect for creating a peaceful and introspective atmosphere. Blue, known for its soothing energy, encourages relaxation and is ideal for kitchens and spaces that you would like to "cool down" a little and bring a sense of tranquillity to.

When used thoughtfully, Water colours help create a space that feels peaceful, reflective and effortlessly flowing. I love the energy that the Water element brings – think of how you feel when you stand next to the ocean: it brings depth, intuition and a sense of flow. However, too much of it can make a space seem overwhelming and heavy, and even leave you feeling a little lost. An excess of blues and blacks might create an emotional weight that leads to feelings of being unmotivated, drained or disconnected from your surroundings. If your home starts to feel too dark, cold or isolating, it's a sign that Water energy has taken over. The way to balance this is to warm the energy up a bit with Earth tones such as creams and beiges to ground the energy or hints of Fire colours like reds and oranges to bring a sense of warmth and to wake the space up a little.

Of course, you don't have to fully redecorate your home to incorporate these elements and colours to bring balance, as you can use simple decorative items instead. Throughout the book I share some suggestions about how you can easily do this, particularly in Part Two: The Room-by-Room Guides, which I'll come to next.

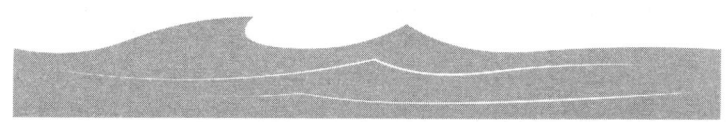

PART TWO

THE ROOM-BY-ROOM GUIDES

CHAPTER 5

HARMONIOUS KITCHENS

There are two good reasons why we want to look after the energy in the kitchen. First, because I'm sure you want to bring harmony into the home and reduce the tension in what can be the busiest room, but second, because in Feng Shui the kitchen isn't just the place where we cook – it represents prosperity, abundance and nourishment in the home. Food symbolizes wealth and vitality, so the energy in your kitchen plays a huge role in supporting both your health and financial well-being.

The kitchen is often described as the heart of the home, but it can also be one of the more tense areas. It's where you try to concentrate on cooking, where everyone tends to gather and where clutter accumulates. It's almost like the kitchen work surface has a magnet for all the bags, water bottles, keys, and stray items in the home. Not only that, but the kitchen is also considered a fiery room in Feng Shui. Historically, the oven brought in a lot of energy, and over time, we've added more Fire energy with electrical appliances – toasters, kettles, ovens, fridges, dishwashers, air fryers – the list goes on! Even though we can't see this energy, we can definitely feel it.

Creating a Kitchen that Attracts Abundance

One of the biggest wealth magnets in the kitchen is the stove. In Feng Shui, the stove symbolizes financial flow, opportunity and success. To allow this energy to come through, the stove needs to be kept clean, and make sure that you use all the burners regularly (instead of just one or two) because this activates the money-making potential in the home and will help to attract more opportunities. A clean, well-maintained stove also keeps the energy fresh and encourages a steady flow of abundance. But here's the magical tip – when you clean the stove, think about welcoming more money into your home. Believe it or not, I've had nearly 100 people message me after posting a reel on this, saying they received unexpected money – from lottery wins to tax rebates!

Here's one of the messages I received, from Layla:

"I gave my stove a deep clean over the weekend, focusing on intentions of money, prosperity and abundance flowing into my life. The very next day, work called to tell me I had been underpaid, and I was getting over £500 back that Friday! I was completely blown away and just had to share my luck."

Enhancing Prosperity in Your Kitchen

Once the stove is clean and wealth energy can enter, it's important that this energy circulates around the kitchen and flows throughout your home. If your kitchen is cluttered, it makes it harder for energy to move. In fact, the energy may get stuck, and you might feel this stagnation in your finances too. Keep your kitchen work surface as clear as possible, and if space is limited, use a small basket with a lid to store stray items.

Traditionally, having plenty of food was a sign of security and wealth, so the kitchen naturally represents your ability to provide, attract and sustain prosperity. Keeping it organized, clutter-free and full of fresh, nourishing ingredients enhances this energy and invites good fortune into your life.

If you're thinking about changing the décor, consider adding a mirrored backsplash to your stove as it symbolically doubles wealth energy. However, be cautious because mirrors double whatever they reflect. If you detest cooking, seeing this reflection all the time might amplify that feeling!

Make sure that you fix any dripping taps or leaking drains – they're not just annoying but are also said to symbolize financial loss. A little maintenance goes a long way in keeping the good energy (and money) flowing in your home.

Managing Tension in the Kitchen

Tension in the kitchen can be caused by the positioning of the stove and sink. The sink has the opposite energy of the stove and pulls energy downward. If your stove and sink are opposite each other, this can create a whirlpool effect of spinning energy, which may lead to friction or arguments. The fix? Add something green between the stove and the sink as this represents the Wood element, which grounds and balances the energy. A simple plant near the stove or a green tea towel draped over the sink can work wonders.

Do you have a knife block? These sharp items could be energetically "stabbing" your relationships, especially if your kitchen is in the Southwest (the relationship area of your home). Simply storing knives in a drawer can make a big difference. One lady, Kavita, shared the following outcome.

"Oh my goodness, Kimberley! I sent our knife block packing to the charity shop at the weekend. Although my husband finds it a little frustrating to open a drawer for the knives, I can't tell you how much calmer the kitchen feels."

The Best Colours for a Harmonious Kitchen

As the kitchen is naturally a fiery room, decorating it with fiery colours (reds, yellows, oranges or purples) can intensify this energy. If your kitchen feels too intense, consider cooling it down with calming blues (representing the Water element) or grounding greens (Wood element). Neutral tones linked to the Earth element also help create a more balanced and peaceful space.

Good lighting is essential. During the day, let in as much natural light as possible to lift the mood and keep everything fresh. In the evening, layering lighting with dimmer switches and candles keeps the space cosy but functional. Avoid harsh lighting that feels glaring or overly dim lighting that makes the room dull – balance is key.

Keeping the Energy Flowing

Fix any broken appliances or utensils as they carry stagnant energy and can weigh down the space. A well-maintained kitchen feels fresh and full of good energy, while broken items can symbolize neglect or stagnation – definitely not the energy you want for wealth!

If your kitchen is part of an open floor plan, create a sense of separation using plants, rugs or furniture to define the space.

Be mindful of keeping bins covered to prevent negative energy from spreading. I take my bin out daily, as small habits like this help maintain a fresh, organized and positive space.

Finally, cook with love and gratitude. The energy you put into preparing meals affects how you feel and the overall atmosphere in your home. If possible, create a cooking ritual – play calming music, light a candle and enjoy the process. It makes a huge difference!

Kitchen Design Tips for Feng Shui Balance

If you're designing or renovating your kitchen, consider these Feng Shui-friendly design features.

◆ Avoid placing the kitchen in the Centre of the home, as this can lead to burnout and health issues.
◆ Avoid positioning the kitchen below a bathroom as this can drain wealth energy – adding plants can help balance this effect.

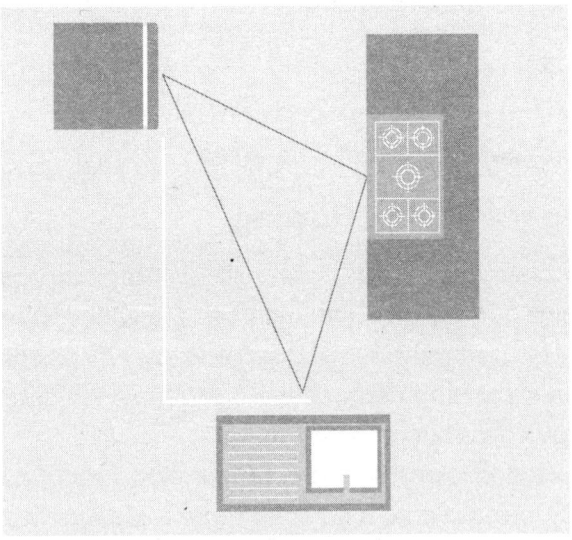

Figure 10. The "kitchen triangle" of fridge, stove and sink.

- Use the "kitchen triangle" layout (fridge, stove and sink forming a triangle) to prevent energy whirlpools (see figure 10).
- Ideally, the stove should not face a wall but be placed in a "command position" (for example, on an island), so you can see the room while cooking.
- Keep knives in a drawer instead of on the countertop to maintain calm energy.

Your kitchen is like the secret wealth weapon of your home because it holds so much energy for prosperity and harmony. With a few simple tweaks of keeping it clean, clutter-free and balanced you can turn it into a magnet for wealth and well-being.

Harmonious Kitchen Checklist

Enhancing Prosperity

- ☑ Keep the stove clean to activate wealth energy
- ☑ Use all burners on the stove regularly to attract financial opportunities
- ☑ Set an intention for abundance when cleaning the stove
- ☑ Clear clutter from countertops to allow energy to flow
- ☑ Store stray items in a basket with a lid
- ☑ Consider a mirrored backsplash behind the stove (but only if you enjoy cooking)
- ☑ Fix dripping taps or leaking drains to prevent financial loss

Reducing Tension

- ☑ If the stove and sink face each other, add a green element (plant or tea towel)
- ☑ Store knives in a drawer instead of a knife block
- ☑ Use neutral, green, or blue tones for a calming effect
- ☑ Ensure the kitchen has good natural and artificial lighting
- ☑ Avoid harsh lighting or overly dim lighting

Keeping Energy Flowing

- ☑ Fix or replace broken appliances
- ☑ If your kitchen is part of an open floor plan, define the space with plants, rugs or furniture
- ☑ Keep bins covered and take out the trash daily
- ☑ Maintain a cooking ritual (music, candle or mindful presence)

Kitchen Design Tips

- ☑ Avoid placing the kitchen in the Centre of the home
- ☑ If the kitchen is below a bathroom, balance energy with plants
- ☑ Follow the kitchen triangle layout (stove, fridge and sink in a triangle)
- ☑ Ensure the stove is in a command position (not facing a wall)
- ☑ Keep knives stored away for a peaceful atmosphere

Things to Avoid

- ☑ Dripping taps or dirty fixtures (symbolize wasted money)
- ☑ Cluttered countertops (keep only daily-use items)
- ☑ Overhead pot racks or floral arrangements blocking energy flow
- ☑ Artificial or dried flowers (create stagnant energy)
- ☑ Expired food in cupboards (check old, dried herbs and spices)

CHAPTER 6
VERSATILE LIVING ROOMS

The living room is where we go to relax, switch off from the day and put our feet up; it's a space for the whole household to come together and enjoy quality time. However, living rooms or family rooms are normally one of the busiest and most social areas in the home, so they are not necessarily the most relaxing! That's why it's important to make sure the energy in these spaces feels balanced – you want it to be cosy enough for winding down but to still have enough energy that you aren't going to fall asleep within five minutes of sitting down!

Shifting the Energy for Different Uses

Think about how you use this room and how you want to feel here. Is it your go-to place at night to relax in? Or is it a base during the day for work/play/exercising? If your living room is mostly for relaxing, then you need to focus on making it as calm and cosy as possible. But let's be honest – most family rooms are super active during the day, especially if you have young children, or you may work from your living room too. If that's the case in your home, I have some really easy suggestions for how you can shift the energy from a bright and lively "Yang" energy during the day to a softer, more peaceful "Yin" atmosphere in the evening.

Arranging Your Furniture for Comfort and Connection

First, we need to look at the furniture layout in the room. It should be arranged in a way that invites conversation and connection. If you can, set up the seating in a circle or semi-circle, as this is a great way to make sure everyone feels included and can easily chat with each other. If chairs are opposite each other, it can feel like you are being interviewed, which is not relaxing at all. Think of how they arrange the seats on morning TV shows compared to how they lay out the seats for a serious documentary. Morning TV invites relaxation and conversation, whereas documentary-style interviews, with the seats opposite each other, have been arranged to make the interviewee feel under pressure.

If possible, avoid having the back of your sofa facing the main door, as this can create a feeling of vulnerability or anxiety simply because you can't see what's coming from behind you, but also because the back of the sofa may stop the flow of positive energy coming into the room – it's a bit like a wall where the energy has to work really hard to get around it. If that's not possible, don't worry. You can soften the feeling by placing a coffee table or a few plants behind the sofa. This not only helps create a sense of security but also keeps the energy flowing smoothly and makes the space feel more grounded. The best option would be to have a solid wall behind the sofa to give the person who sits there a sense of support.

A little Feng Shui tip is to leave a few inches of space between the sofa and the wall as well. This small gap lets the energy flow freely around you, preventing it from getting stuck.

Amanda Hawes suggests incorporating flexible furniture arrangements in neurodiverse households, such as movable seating or modular storage. This allows for different preferences, whether it's sitting, lying down, having an armrest or sitting in a corner, so everyone can relax in their own way.

Avoiding Harsh Angles and Sharp Corners

When arranging your furniture, try to avoid sharp angles like the corner of a coffee table or edges of a table pointing toward the seating area (see figure 11). These sharp angles, known as "poison arrows" in Feng Shui (the terminology is so harsh!), can create quite an uncomfortable energy – a little like how you feel when someone points their finger at you – and it can disrupt the flow of energy in the room. Basically, sharp angles can make the space feel tense or stressful. If you can, position your furniture to keep those angles away from the main seating spots; but if you can't move the furniture, you can add plants or soft cushions to soften the energy and make the space feel calmer and more inviting.

If you are ready to change your furniture (and this includes tables, sofas, chairs and even rugs), go for items with softer, rounder edges. Interestingly, I feel that this is becoming more of a trend in interior design, where more people are moving away from clean and crisp lines and instead using curvature to create a lovely flow throughout the home.

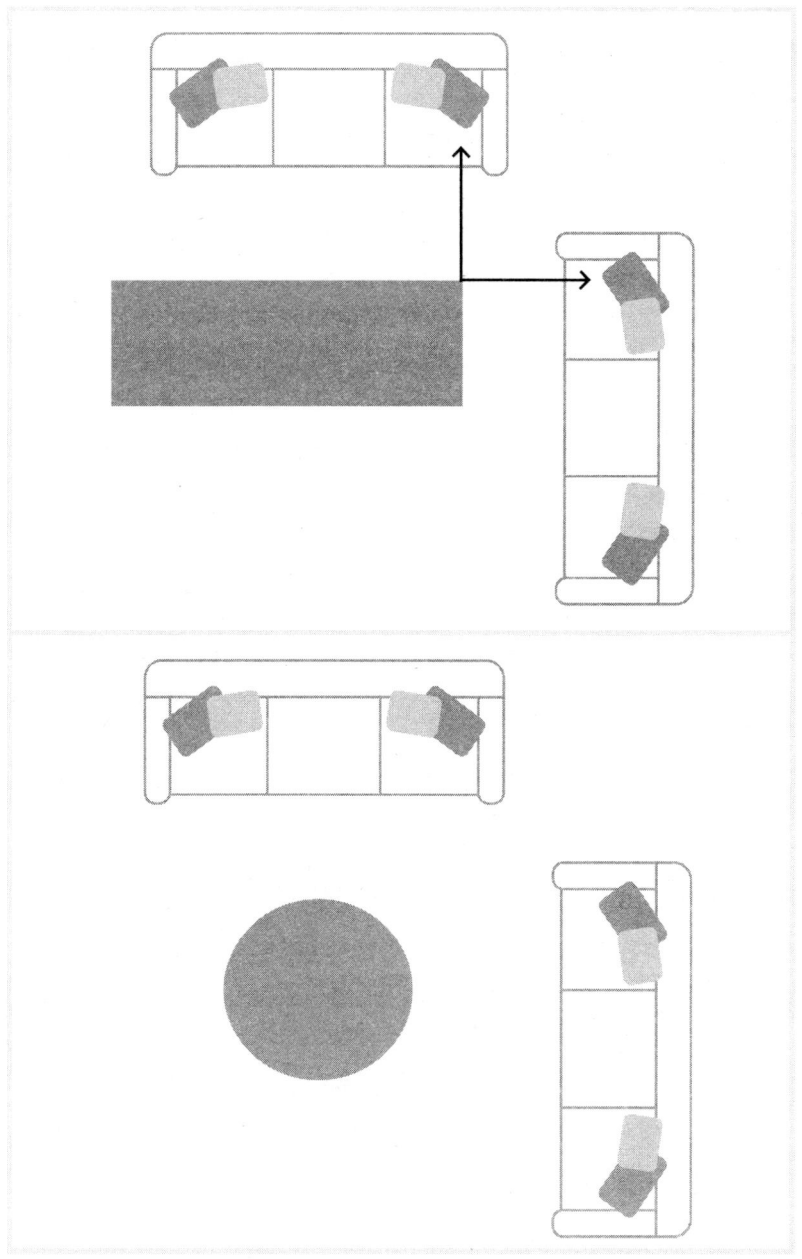

Figure 11. How the corners of the table at the top could be impacting people sitting on the sofas, compared to a round table below, which doesn't have the sharp angles.

Have a look where the lighting is in the room too, because sitting directly beneath spotlights can create quite an uncomfortable, pressured feeling that won't help people relax at all.

Keeping the Space Open and Clutter-Free

Keeping your living space clean and clutter-free is key to letting good energy flow freely around the room: when there's too much stuff around, it can block the flow and make the room feel chaotic. Try not to overcrowd the room with furniture or decorative items because less is often more. I worked with a lady who asked me to visit her home and she said that people don't often relax when they come over. It was a busy household with lots of visitors, but no one ever sat down and instead gathered around in the kitchen. What was interesting was that she had numerous sofas and seats in the living room, but that was actually the problem. It was overcrowded and people found it hard to relax there. So, the first thing we did was take some of the sofas away, which created a lot more space for everyone, and before I had even left, people had moved from the kitchen and were relaxing on the sofas – including the dogs!

Supporting Neurodiverse Household Members

For those who are neurodiverse, having their own seat is really important. When I was a teacher, I would let the students choose their seat on the first day, and then that was "their" seat for the rest of the year. This gives people (especially children) a sense of personal space and control, which can help reduce anxiety and make the environment feel less overwhelming. It's all about having a spot that works for them where they can avoid sensory overload, such as bright lights or noise, and will therefore feel more comfortable. Having their own seat also helps set boundaries and allows individuals with neurodiversity to manage social situations on their own terms, making everything feel a little more manageable and less stressful. It also allows individuals to add or remove items around them that make them feel more comfortable – a weighted blanket is a great addition if they struggle to sit down and relax. It's a really simple way to create a more supportive and relaxed atmosphere for everyone in the home.

However, I do understand that changing environments can be daunting when you are neurodiverse. I worked with a lady who had two very high-functioning neurodiverse children who really struggled with some of the colours I asked her to add to her home. I never ask people to add permanent features and instead use decorative items, such as cushions or throws, but this meant that the children would actively move them. However, she sat down with her children and explained why they were there and they agreed not to move them. After this, she said she noticed a real improvement in the areas they were all struggling with. It really is worth trying to explain to everyone in the home what you are trying to achieve and ask them how they feel when they sit down to relax, what they like and dislike about the room, and work together to create a space for everyone.

To help create a more Yin and relaxed feeling at night, you will need to find a home for all of the extra items in the living room such as toys, electronics, work items or workout equipment. Storage doesn't have to cost a fortune either and I often recommend laundry baskets with lids on (to keep the energy enclosed) as a way of hiding all the clutter and keeping things neat. This way, you'll have a calm, organized space where the energy feels balanced, and the whole room just feels a lot more relaxing.

Using Colour to Set the Mood

When choosing colours for the living room, it's important to pick shades that help you feel more relaxed. Neutral tones like soft beiges, greys and whites are great for making the area feel nice and calm. If you are looking to add more colour, then greens are wonderful, as they represent the Wood element and will bring grounding to the room. Personally, I would avoid too much blue in the living room because, although it is a relaxing colour, it can actually introduce a sense of sadness and feeling low (think of the phrase "I've got the blues"). Metallic colours like gold and silver are also good to add because they help to absorb negative energy, which will also promote relaxation.

Lighting

Make the most of natural light during the day by letting it fill the room because this brings a lovely new energy with it. Open the curtains or blinds and let the sunshine in even if you don't use this room in the daytime. Natural light has such a positive effect on our mood and the energy in the home, and it helps the space feel open and airy. When it comes to the evening, you want to be able to change the energy back to being more relaxed. It's like doing a "nighttime turn-down service" in your home (but perhaps without the added skill of being able to turn a towel into a swan!).

Layered lighting in the evening really helps to create a cosy, inviting feeling. Think about using a mix of floor lamps, table lamps, and dimmers to control the mood. This way, you can adjust the lighting to suit the energy you want in the room. The idea is that any light below eye level represents the sun setting, so it helps you to unwind at the end of the day.

Amanda Hawes shared her top neurodiverse-friendly lighting recommendations

◆ Using dimmable lights and warm-toned LED bulbs
◆ Hanging blackout curtains to control light levels when needed
◆ Having low-level lighting, such as lamps, to create the feel of sunset and relaxation
◆ Including lighting that mimics natural elements, such as salt lamps as they are known to enhance relaxation and grounding
◆ Providing lighting options that are layered, such as combining table lamps, floor lamps, overhead dimmable lighting and string lights in a room. Options such as these allow for flexibility in creating a sensory-friendly environment for everyone in the home with varying needs. This approach ensures that the lighting can be adjusted to suit different activities, such as reading and relaxing, reducing sensory overload or winding down before bedtime.
◆ Incorporating as much natural light through windows or skylights to support the natural regulation of circadian rhythms or your biological clock, as well as to boost natural levels of serotonin

(mood-balancing chemical) **and
dopamine** (reward chemical) **within
the brain
Each of these is essential for quality sleep
and overall boosting of well-being and
the creation of a calm home environment.**
(Figueiro et al., 2017).

The Power of Personal Touches and Artwork

A nice way to personalize your living room is to include family photos, artwork or meaningful décor that brings you joy and happiness. This helps to make the room feel warmer and more relaxing and if you feel there is a disconnect in your family, adding family photos will help to bring a feeling of togetherness into the home. However, remember to remove photos of family members or friends whom you don't actually like! (see pages 43/56). I remember when my husband and I got married, our photographer told us not to worry about having photos with people we didn't like on the day because she could just photoshop them out afterwards! So, either learn how to use photoshop or remove their pictures!

Once you have decided which family members are allowed into your living room, remember that you can place them anywhere apart from above the fireplace as previously discussed (see page 43).

Please also be mindful of the artwork in your home. In Feng Shui, abstract art isn't always seen as the best choice because it can feel a bit unclear or confusing. The idea is that art should be something that brings balance and harmony to the space, and when you can't really recognize what is happening in the picture, it can leave you feeling a little unsettled or uncertain.

That said, it really depends on the piece. If the colours, shapes or energy of the artwork make you feel good and bring a sense of calm or inspiration, then it can totally work. I have a lovely abstract piece behind me when I work because I like the flow of the paint and the calming colours in it. The most important thing is to choose art that feels right for you and enhances the energy you are trying to create in your home.

Using Mirrors Mindfully

Mirrors are a really powerful tool in Feng Shui because they can help to "double up" light and energy, making a room feel brighter and more spacious. Nonetheless, it's important to be mindful of where you place them. Avoid positioning mirrors where they reflect clutter, the front door or windows. Reflecting clutter can cause the energy to feel chaotic, as it draws attention to the mess, making the area feel even less calm. Placing a mirror where it reflects the front door or windows can cause the energy to bounce right back out of the room, which can make the room feel quite stagnant.

Ensuring Energy Can Enter Freely

The most important thing is that the energy can enter the living room easily. The entrance is where energy (or Chi) flows into the space, so you want to make sure there's nothing blocking it. This means keeping the area clear of clutter, furniture or anything else that could get in the way of the flow of energy. You want the space to feel open and accessible, setting a good tone for the whole room. It's also super important that the door can open easily to allow the energy to enter, and that the door handle is sturdy and not wobbly, as this can represent instability and a lack of control in life.

Creating a balanced and relaxing living room is all about finding the right mix of comfort, energy and flow. By arranging your furniture to encourage connection, softening harsh angles and adapting the atmosphere to suit different times of the day, you can transform your space into one that feels both inviting and calming. Small adjustments, like adding plants, adjusting lighting or shifting furniture slightly can make a big difference in how the room feels. Ultimately, your living room should support your lifestyle, whether it's a lively gathering space during the day or a peaceful retreat in the evening.

Living Room Checklist

Balancing Energy for Different Uses

☑ Define how you use the space (daytime activity vs evening relaxation)
☑ Use brighter lighting and active colours for daytime energy
☑ Dim lights and incorporate soft textures for a calming evening atmosphere

Arranging Furniture for Comfort and Connection

☑ Set up seating in a circular or semi-circular layout to encourage conversation
☑ Avoid placing the back of the sofa facing the room entrance (or soften with a table or plants)

☑ Leave a small gap between the sofa and the wall for energy flow

Minimizing Harsh Angles and Sharp Corners

☑ Soften "poison arrows" (sharp furniture edges) with plants, cushions or more curved furniture
☑ Avoid sitting directly under harsh spotlights

Keeping the Space Open and Clutter-free

☑ Remove unnecessary furniture to allow energy to flow freely
☑ Use stylish storage solutions (for example, baskets with lids) to keep clutter out of sight

Supporting Neurodiverse Household Members

☑ Provide a designated seat for comfort and security
☑ Create a sensory-friendly environment with soft lighting, textures and weighted blankets

Using Colour to Set the Mood

☑ Choose neutral and earthy tones for a relaxing atmosphere
☑ Incorporate greens for grounding energy
☑ Avoid excessive blues, which can feel overly cold

Layering Lighting for a Cosy Atmosphere

☑ Maximize natural light during the day
☑ Use a mix of floor lamps, table lamps and dimmers for evening relaxation
☑ Position lighting below eye level for a soothing effect

Incorporating Personal Touches and Meaningful Décor

☑ Display family photos and artwork that bring joy and connection
☑ Avoid artwork with unsettling or chaotic energy
☑ Place mirrors thoughtfully to reflect light but not clutter

Ensuring Energy Flows Freely

☑ Keep doorways clear of obstructions to let energy enter smoothly
☑ Ensure the door handle to the room is sturdy

CHAPTER 7

DELIGHTFUL DINING ROOMS

The dining room isn't just where we eat; it's a space for connecting with others and creating a sense of harmony in the home. Feng Shui can help transform your dining room into a place that feels balanced and inviting. By paying attention to the layout, the furniture arrangement and the décor, you can create a dining space that encourages good vibes, open conversations and an enjoyable mealtime experience.

The Dining Table

As well as the dining table's obvious practical use, in Feng Shui it also symbolically represents nourishment, unity and abundance in the home. What if I told you that by making a few adjustments and adding some elements to your dining table and the area around it, you could have peaceful and enjoyable family dinners every night? How lovely would that be? Well, it is possible and here is how you can achieve this.

Do you use your dining table to work on? I quite often do this and sometimes my daughter does her homework there too, which is totally fine, but just make sure that at the end of the day and when it's time to eat, you put everything away. Having work items on or surrounding the table can create an energy of exhaustion, so if your dining experience with your family saps your energy, it may be worth checking what is around you when you eat.

There are a few things to consider when you are thinking about where to put the dining table. If it can be placed in the centre of the room, that is perfect because everyone can access their seat easily and it allows the good energy to flow freely around the space, making the room feel balanced and inviting. When the room is energetically balanced, people will naturally feel more relaxed and be less tempted to argue or leave as soon as the meal is over. I think communication is so important in the home, and the dining table is the perfect place for this. When we lived in the UK, we never ate together just because of everyone's different activities. But as soon as we moved to Australia, we knew that communication was going to get us through the first few tricky months, and so we made a pact to sit down together every evening to eat dinner, and I truly believe it helped us so much as a family.

One thing to try to do if you live in a warm country, is to avoid placing the dining table directly under a ceiling fan. While this makes perfect sense practically, ceiling fans can stir and chop up the energy, which can make the space feel a little chaotic and the people restless at the table. If you do have a fan above your table, I would just turn it off at mealtimes. And if you have the option of designing your space from scratch, I would offset the fan slightly so that you still benefit from it, but it won't disrupt the energy.

Choosing a Dining Table

The best shape for a table is round or oval because, if you think about the shape, these promote equality as no one really has the "dominant position" (the head-of-table position). This can be a huge benefit for family dynamics. Also, sharp corners on square or rectangular tables can create quite a harsh energy that may lead to tension around the table. Having said that, it can be quite difficult to have a round table due to the layout of rooms, so if you have to have a square- or rectangular-shaped table, try to choose one that has rounded corners and add softer décor such as a table runner or a tablecloth to the table top. Our dining table couldn't be more un-Feng-Shui-friendly if it tried. Not only is it rectangular in shape with super sharp corners, it's made of concrete, so it's really harsh. If you have a similar table, you can soften this energy by adding some plants to the centre – choose ones that have soft green leaves like a "money plant", because these will help to ground the energy around the table.

Table Settings

Now for the more fun part, in my opinion – the table settings. Believe it or not, the plates, dishes and bits and bobs on the table can impact the energy in the room. Feng Shui is all about simplicity and balance. Therefore, having matching plates, bowls and cutlery will help to achieve this feeling. Moreover, there is something so lovely about seeing a table laid beautifully. Symmetry is really important on the table, because this also helps to achieve the balance of energy, and it also shows that everyone around it is equal, which helps people to relax and be far more open to communicating.

Now, let's talk about something we're all probably guilty of – hanging on to chipped plates, cracked bowls or bent utensils because "they still work". I get it, but in Feng Shui, these little imperfections can cause an edginess in the energy. They carry a subtle message of lack or incompleteness, which is not what you want in a space meant to nurture and uplift! If you've got a favourite plate with a tiny chip or a glass that's seen better days, it might be time to say goodbye to it. Think of it as clearing out the old to make way for fresh, positive energy. It doesn't mean that you have to go out and buy expensive tableware but, it's best to go for quality over quantity. It doesn't mean that your table must look like a Michelin Star restaurant either. It can still be fun and you can add things like table runners, colourful napkins and textured placemats – just try to avoid it looking cluttered so that the energy can flow freely around the table.

Balancing Personalities at the Table

When it comes to seating positions around the dining table, you need to decide who sits at the head of the table for several reasons. You want to create the command position for them, which means that they should ideally face the door. When this person can see the door, it makes them feel a lot more comfortable because they can also see everything in front of them and who is entering the room. It's almost as if they are in charge of the space, and this can give the person a sense of calm and confidence. But just be careful about who you give this position to – it can be your secret! If someone is outgoing and bordering on the egotistical, I would perhaps place them with their back to the door, because this will slightly diminish their authority and command of the room. Then, if you have someone in your household who is a little quiet, I would consider giving them the command position to give their confidence a boost.

I worked with a lady called Zhara who had two children who were polar opposites. One was super confident and would sit and chat happily, thoroughly enjoying mealtimes. But the other was quiet and shy, to the point where they hardly said anything at all and would want to leave the table as soon as they had eaten. So, we had a look at who sat where around the table and moved the quieter child to the "command position". Over time, Zhara could not believe the difference in how much they interacted at mealtimes. The quieter child became so much chattier and more fun. It's definitely worth thinking carefully about who sits in what position around the table and allocating their places according to their personality.

Some people find it quite a struggle to sit at the table when eating, and this is really common for those who are neurodiverse, whether that's because of the length of time they are expected to be there, or because of the sensory overload from the sounds of cooking and the smells and sight of food. If this resonates with you, then I would also make sure that they aren't in the direct line of the door. The theory is that there's a chance the energy will shoot straight into the room at speed (remember I mentioned how energy takes the path of least resistance and that it loves traveling in straight lines (see page 53). And this can feel quite overwhelming for whoever is in line with it as they will feel the constant flow of energy coming directly at them. If you can't move the table, placing a plant in between the table and the door will help to reduce the impact on the person who is in line with the door.

Selecting Colours

When choosing colours for the dining room, you want to pick them from a variety of the elements because this will help you create a lovely energetic balance between Yin and Yang in the room. You need the space to feel calm and relaxed but also have enough energy, so that people communicate with each other and have fun – especially if you entertain in this space as well.

Earthy tones, such as creams and beiges are good because they help to ground the energy in the space and promote a sense of stability. These colours are closely tied to the Earth element in Feng Shui, which is grounding, calm and supportive. However, I would also encourage you to add some colour, like sage green or muted yellows, because these hues will bring a soft liveliness to the room without it feeling overwhelming. It's a bit like putting together ingredients for a recipe – you want a little bit of grounding and calm mixed with some happiness and a little bit of effervescence!

Depending on your family, I would probably try to avoid the brighter fiery colours such as vivid reds because these can induce a feeling of stress and anxiety. Bright reds can be very intense and lead to an imbalance in the energy in the room, making people feel restless and sometimes even quite aggressive. Black can add an element of sophistication, as I mentioned in chapter 4 about balancing colours, but keep it minimal, as it can make the room feel quite draining. This area is meant to have a light, social and positive energy, so if you love to add bolder colours in your home, I would go for neutral tones with accents of colour, rather than painting entire walls in, say, bright red!

Lighting and Mirrors

Good lighting plays a crucial role in creating calm and happy spaces in the home. When it comes to the dining room, it's even more important. This might be a personal thing, but I really struggle if we go out for a nice meal and the restaurant is too light. It's all I can talk about and it drives my husband mad, but I find it hard to relax when the room is very bright. There's a reason why McDonald's is so cold and bright – it's all done on purpose, so you don't spend too long there! This means the dining room needs to find a balance between the lighting being functional so you can actually see those around you and what you are eating but dim enough for you to relax around the table as well.

During the day, it's important that you allow as much natural light and energy to enter the dining space as possible, and if you have a separate dining room, this is really important because you need to make sure that the energy doesn't stagnate and hold on to any negativity from previous days. So, open the drapes or blinds because this will keep the room alive energetically. Then, in the evening, you can start to bring the lighting down slightly to create a lovely warm and cosy atmosphere. Candles are great for the dining table because they create the perfect level of lighting and they also help to burn off negative energy. If you find your family dining experience is slightly too lively (to put it politely), dimming the lights will work well to help calm the room and lower everyone's personal energy levels, too.

Mirrors in the dining room can be a fantastic way to enhance the space. Nevertheless, there needs to be a balance between creating a positive energy flow and an energetic whirlwind that will disrupt the atmosphere of the room. There are a few things to take into consideration before adding mirrors. When used correctly they can encourage wealth and prosperity because they can amplify the flow of positive energy. But I would advise you not to hang a mirror where it directly reflects the dining table, because this can promote a feeling of overwhelm or even lead to overeating due to the constant reflection of the food on the table.

Instead, you want to encourage more light and openness in the room. If there are dark corners in the room, you can use mirrors to help light up these areas. Or, they can reflect something positive, such as lovely photos or artwork. The shape of the mirror is also important, and I would suggest having one with a rounded or an oval frame because this brings a much softer energy to the room. Keeping the mirror clean and free from fingerprints and smudges will really help the energy as dirty mirrors can block the flow of positive energy.

The Power of Music at Mealtimes

Playing lovely music at dinner time will help to calm the energy around the table. Music has been scientifically proved to reduce cortisol levels, reduce your heart rate and stimulate the feel-good hormone dopamine. Music can be most helpful for people who are neurodivergent because it helps the brain to support emotional regulation, communication and sensory processing, all of which will help them relax around the dining table. When I was a teacher, I learned that music tuned to 432Hz (Hz are the frequency of sound waves) has been proved to help calm and relax people. As soon as you know which songs this relates to, you will understand – and they aren't all slow and boring! Some examples of 432Hz songs:

- *Wonderwall* by Oasis
- *Blinding Lights* by The Weekend
- *Titanium* by David Guetta and Sia
- *Californication* by Red Hot Chilli Peppers
- *Your Song* by Elton John
- *Dancing in the Dark* by Bruce Springsteen
You can search for 432Hz music wherever you stream your

music and there are plenty of playlists – I'm currently writing this while listening to these!

The Effect of Artwork

Artwork can have a big impact on the energy of your dining space, so it's important to really think about what surrounds you when you sit down to eat as a family. The most ideal artwork would be anything that means "wealth and abundance" to you and your family, family photos and anything else that brings you joy and happiness. These will lift your mood when you see them, which will help to bring a more positive energy to the dinner table. If you feel that your dining table is lacking in communication, choose art that includes flowing water, lovely bright flowers or vibrant wildlife because these symbolize life and moving energy. Your aim is to create more flow and growth in the room, and these will help to bring that energy into the space. I would avoid artwork that shows anything negative, such as stormy skies because this could encourage "stormy" energy; similarly, I wouldn't recommend images of anyone by themselves because this may result in people feeling isolated. I think we often choose artwork because a wall needs to be filled, rather than really thinking about what energy the picture is bringing to the room. We have lots of pictures of the Amalfi Coast in our dining room, because one day I would love to go there – preferably on a massive yacht! Feel free to get in touch if you can help me with this!

Remember, your dining room is about so much more than just eating. It's where you come together as a family, connect and share your day with the people you care about, so it's really worth giving some time and making an effort to make it as pleasant a room as possible. .

Delightful Dining Room Checklist

Choosing the Right Table

- ☑ Round or oval tables help people feel equal and connected
- ☑ If you have a rectangular table, soften the edges with a tablecloth or plants

Preparing the Table

- ☑ Remove work, homework and clutter before meals to create a peaceful space
- ☑ Place the table in the middle of the room for good energy flow
- ☑ Avoid putting the table under a ceiling fan to prevent unsettled energy

Picking Table Settings and Crockery

- ☑ Use matching plates and cutlery to create balance
- ☑ Get rid of any chipped or broken crockery, as it brings bad energy
- ☑ Arrange table settings evenly to make everyone feel valued

Arranging Seating for Comfort and Balance

- ☑ Let the person in charge sit facing the door for confidence

☑ Give introverted or sensitive people a seat where they feel comfortable

Selecting Room Colours and Decorations

☑ Choose warm colours like soft green or light yellow for a cosy feel
☑ Avoid too much red, which can cause stress or arguments
☑ Hang happy artwork, avoiding sad or lonely images

Choosing Good Lighting and Background Music

☑ Maximize natural light during the day to brighten the space
☑ Use soft lights or candles at night to create a calm mood
☑ Play soft, relaxing music to make meals feel pleasant

Positioning Mirrors and Ensuring Energy Flow

☑ Don't place a mirror facing the table directly, as it can feel overwhelming
☑ Use mirrors to reflect light or positive images

CHAPTER 8
CALMING CHILDREN'S BEDROOMS

One of the most rewarding parts of what I do is help children feel happier and calmer in the home. When I was a teacher, I became aware of how the classroom impacted the energy of the students, especially as many of them were neurodiverse and just being at college was difficult enough. Traditional learning environments of rows of seats, rote learning, reading huge amounts of text, speaking in front of their peers – it was just one challenge after another.

I learned along the way that the colours of the classroom impacted how children behaved, as did the seating arrangements, and even the noise and smell changed the energy. At the beginning of every session, I would arrange the chairs so that everyone was comfortable. I did this by positioning the desks in a large U shape so that no one had anyone sitting behind them, as this can make people feel uncomfortable. I opened all the windows and used to play calming music in the background – and this was all before I knew anything about Feng Shui. I just knew that a chaotic classroom would undoubtedly cause a chaotic lesson and that was the last thing I needed. Perhaps that's why I'm so passionate about helping children, because I have seen the benefits of creating a calm environment first hand.

Clients often come to me because they want to improve their relationship with their children, or they want their children to get on better. One client, Priya, had two girls who in her words, "fought like cats and dogs", and her husband was always caught in the middle, which brought a lot of tension into the home and their relationship. I analysed her home and sent over the report. Within a few weeks this was her email response: "Who would have guessed that by adding some elements to my home it would make my house feel like it's supporting me, my family and the business. The girls are getting on so much better, which means that my husband and I can actually have a conversation together in the evening instead of preventing a war breaking out upstairs!"

I totally get that it doesn't make logical sense that just adding and changing a few items around your home can make such a difference. But I do believe that something like Feng Shui, which has been practised for more than 4,000 years, must offer some truth and wisdom.

Neurodesign for Children's Bedrooms

I asked Amanda Hawes about how we can best design bedrooms for neurodiverse children, and here are her recommendations.

"Textures such as soft fabrics, weighted blankets or weighted animals, or smooth and cuddly surfaces, can provide sensory comfort, particularly for individuals with autism or anxiety. Natural materials like wood or cotton can also create a grounding effect, increasing a connection to nature, which has been shown to improve well-being (Capaldi et al., 2015). It is very important to be able to personalize these elements to yourself or family members in creating a supportive and calm environment. This is particularly important after a busy day at school or socializing, when someone is trying very hard to calm their senses and manage in a world that feels loud, bright, smelly, scratchy, changeable and unpredictable."

As we know, the purpose of Feng Shui is to make spaces feel good and to aid energy to flow in a positive way. Creating a calm and structured environment is essential for supporting neurodiverse children, as it helps reduce anxiety and improve focus (National Library of Medicine, 2022). When their space is organized and has the right colours, furniture and decorations in the right places, it can encourage neurodiverse children's brain to feel less busy and more peaceful. This means they can sleep better, play happily and feel safe, which is all we can really ask for as parents.

The tricky part is that a child's bedroom isn't just for sleeping in. It's where they also play, do homework and even game, and that energy is totally opposite to what we are aiming for when we want children to wind down at bedtime. Amanda Hawes believes that the multi-functions of the bedroom can make it harder for neurodiverse children to relax. She suggests that we try to create clear boundaries for activities, such as quiet zones, low sensory areas and play and active areas, to help manage sensory sensitivity.

Ten Steps to a Calmer Bedroom

This chapter concentrates mainly on younger children (from toddlers to tweens), because as children get older, they quite rightly have more say in how they organize their own space in the home. However, I have also given some tips along the way that should help teens and older children. The tips I'm sharing are all about helping your child feel better in many different ways. Each little task clears some of the negativity that can leave them feeling unsettled, upset, grumpy or even bouncing off the walls of their room. We want to bring in good energy that fills their space with positive, happy and calm feelings instead.

Step One – Decluttering

Younger Children

By now I'm sure you know the drill – step one is always decluttering, and this time we're tackling your child's bedroom. I know, it probably feels like a massive task and you're gearing up for a battle. But trust me, this is the first step in transforming the energy in that room. So, it's time to roll up your sleeves and start digging through those drawers, pulling out all the forgotten toys and random bits that haven't seen the light of day in ages. Personally, I like to do a good declutter right before Christmas for two reasons. First, it's such a hectic time for everyone, and keeping the energy flowing smoothly at home helps keep things calm. And second, good old Santa is likely to refresh the toy stash with even more over-sized toys. Why is it that the smaller the child, the bigger the toys? I remember our lounge looking like a fairground at one stage!

I also love delving into my daughter's room in the spring. Spring cleaning is a thing for a reason, and in Feng Shui, spring ushers in a wonderful Yang energy – that uplifting feeling you get when the days get longer, warmer and brighter. We want to bring that gorgeous feeling into our homes. However, when my daughter was little, I used to carry out this step when she wasn't around. Even now, if she spots me taking away one of her 567 teddies, it suddenly becomes her absolute favourite, and we can't possibly get rid of it. So, I've learned to declutter in stages. I'll put a few things away in a bag and hide them for a month. If she doesn't notice "Fluffy" has gone missing by then, Fluffy's off to a new home!

Decluttering really helps good energy flow around your child's room. The fewer things in there, the easier it is for that positive energy to circulate, shifting the energy in the room from chaotic to calm in a relatively short period of time. I know that the easy option is to fill their room with toys, because you don't want them clogging up all the other rooms in the house, but quite often the more choices they have, the fewer things they actually play with. It's like going to a restaurant with a massive menu – you're so spoiled for choice that you end up ordering the same thing every time! And don't worry, you can still store toys in their room – I'm not that mean! Just use baskets, boxes or chests with lids to keep them and their energy tucked away neatly.

Teens and Older Children

Getting a teen to declutter when they don't want your help can be difficult because you don't want to nag, but you also may feel you can't ignore the chaos in their room. I would try to let them take the lead. I instead of telling them what to do, ask them how their room feels to them. It needs to be their choice and it's just not worth the argument if they don't want to do it. You could suggest having a "maybe box", in which they can put anything they are unsure about. Then, if they don't touch it for a few months, out it goes.

Decluttering can feel overwhelming, so it may help to set a small goal like clearing one drawer, which is much more manageable. The key is to focus on the benefits and try not to judge. If they want to keep every concert ticket and random souvenir, let them! Decluttering is a process and if they see you leading by example with other areas of the house, they are more likely to follow.

To help with organization, Amanda Hawes suggests that adding visual schedules or labels to items can reduce stress for individuals with ADHD (attention deficit hyperactivity disorder) or autism. Personally, I love a visual schedule, and we have one on our fridge for school activities to help us remember what uniform is needed each day, and what before- and after-school activities are on throughout the week.

Step Two – Deep Cleaning

I know it's not glamorous, but honestly, cleaning your child's bedroom is so important. The thing is, children never complain about their room being dirty or notice if there's dust piling up on the shelves. My daughter's shelves are jam-packed with the most random things, so I have to push myself to get in there and clean.

I totally get that this isn't the easiest job, but a good dusting really makes a difference. I know a lot of people listen to my podcast while they clean because it helps to motivate them (a little self-plug here and it's available on all platforms!). But the reason why we want those surfaces nice and clean is to let good energy glide around the room freely, not get stuck.

Cleaning is cleaning; you don't need me to explain any more about this.

Step Three – The Bed

The bed is the focal point of any bedroom, as the whole point of the bedroom is to sleep in it. However, with children, we tend to cross that line because it is where they also do other things, as previously mentioned, such as play, do homework and game. It's also where we may send them for time-out, so there can be a lot of different energy in this room. Because of this, the room can be filled with a wide range of different emotions, from sadness to playful energy. When you think about it, it's crazy that we then expect them to sleep peacefully in the same space.

Let's focus on the bed in the bedroom for the sake of getting a good night's sleep. Sleep conquers all, so if your child sleeps well, it makes the whole world a brighter place! The first thing to think about is the position of the bed. The ideal situation is what we again call the "command position", where the back of the bed is against a strong wall, or pushed up into a corner. This gives children a feeling of security, so that they can relax and not feel that they have to look over their shoulder. I would avoid having the bed in the middle of the room, which is sometimes how smaller cots are positioned for aesthetics. Take a step back and think about it; if a cot is in the middle of the room, there is a lot of space around the child as it is very open, and this can make them feel a bit lonely and less cosy.

Ideally, the bed would not be underneath a window because windows are not solid, and we don't want children to feel that their surroundings are "fragile". We want to give them strength and support. Having a bed that faces the entrance so they can see the door gives them a feeling of security. It means they don't get that feeling that they have to keep checking for something over their shoulder to see if anything is there. This is a natural position because we want to be able to see everything in front of us.

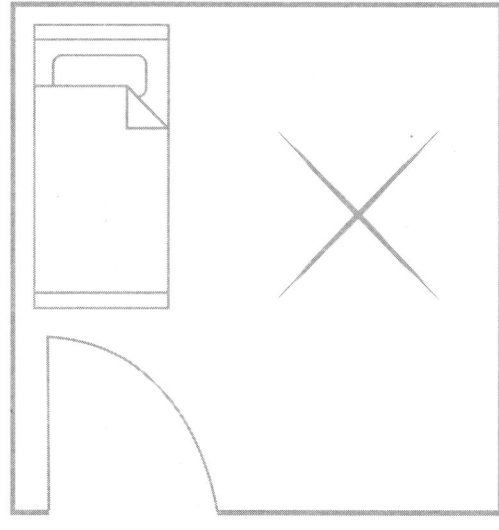

Figure 12 shows the bed in direct line to the door, which isn't advisable because the energy will be coming straight into the room and shooting up the bed. This may impact a child's sleep and could lead to them feeling anxious and irritable.

Figure 12. The bed in direct line with the door

The next image (figure 13) shows the bed against the same wall as the door, which in Feng Shui means that you don't have control of your space. This can lead to feelings of restlessness, lack of security and stress. If this is the only position you can have the

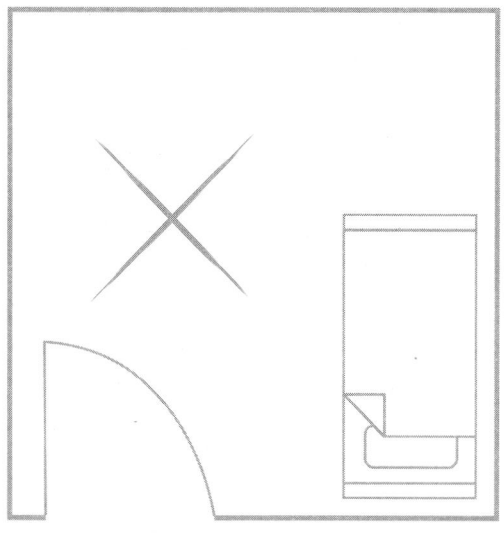

Figure 13. The bed is against the same wall as the door

bed in, you can get a compact mirror or one used in play – It doesn't have to be anything fancy – and angle it so when your child looks at it from their bed they can see the door entrance. You don't even need to tell them why it's there and they may not even notice what you have done. But this is a great way of getting around the issue of bed placement and trying to help your child have a good night's sleep.

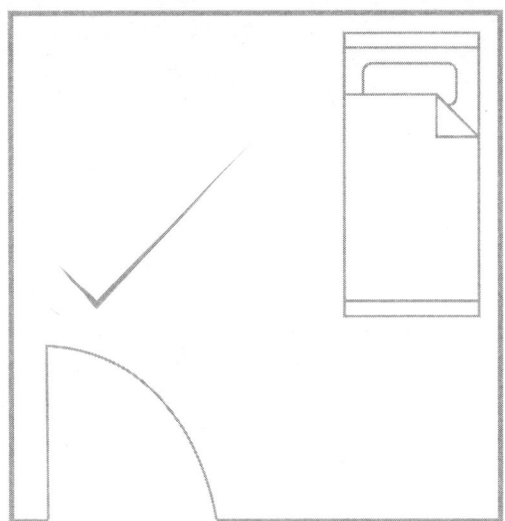

The third image (figure 14) shows the ideal position for a child's bed because it's in the "command position". They can see the door, have command over the room, yet they aren't in a direct line of the energy coming in through the door. According to Feng Shui this helps your child have a sense of security, promotes better sleep and also emotional well-being because they will feel more relaxed.

Figure 14. The bed in the "command position", where the occupant can see the door but is not in a direct line of the energy entering the room.

Finally, if possible, I would steer clear of bunk beds. Whoever is underneath is going to feel the energy pushing down on them from the person or even just the bed above, and this can create a suppressing energy. A friend's child was sleeping on the bottom bunk and suffering from frequent night terrors, so I suggested that she separated the beds to see if that helped. As if by magic, the child only had one or two night terrors in the following six months. I know that bunk beds are amazing for saving space, but if your child is suffering with anything like this, or with anxiety, I strongly recommend you consider separating the beds.

I fully appreciate that all these tips are not always possible – my own daughter's room is far from Feng Shui perfect, so just do what you can and keep it practical.

Step Four – Bedding

What colour is your child's bedding? Does it have something energetic on it like monster trucks or characters with superpowers? I'm not sure when the transition happens, but all bedding for babies tends to be muted, with lovely soft pinks, blues and yellows. Then as soon as they move into their first proper bed, BANG, we get the full range of colours, with all the boundless energy that comes with this!
The aim is to create a feeling of calm in their room, but don't get me wrong (I am not a total killjoy), they may still want an element of play on show. That's fine. But there is a balance between fun and calmness and I would advise getting a softer-coloured duvet cover with nothing crazy on it. If the child absolutely insists (and believe me, I fully understand how insistent little ones can be) then, you could compromise with a throw or blanket to cover up the characters at bedtime.

Weighted blankets are another great idea, especially for neurodiverse children, because they provide a sense of security and calm by applying gentle pressure, which can be really soothing for children with sensory sensitivities.

Step Five – Storage

I totally understand that storage is more often than not an issue with children. Nonetheless, storing items under the bed isn't ideal because this energy can travel up and impact their sleep. If you do need to store things underneath beds, make sure the items are nice and soft, such as tracksuit bottoms, hoodies, bedding and so on. What you don't want to have under the bed are any toys with sharp edges or even battery-powered ones like cars or talking animals. My daughter had this really scary purple unicorn that seemed to have a mind of its own and would make its way around the room by itself. This sort of thing gave me nightmares as a child, yet for some reason I thought it was OK to put it in her room! As soon as I began my Feng Shui journey, it mysteriously disappeared ... along with Fluffy!

Closed storage solutions like an ottoman at the end of the bed are always best so that the toys are not on display when the child is sleeping. Or a laundry bin with a lid on would also do perfectly.

What else is "open" in your child's room? For example, do they have a shoe rack? Ideally, shoes would go in a wardrobe, but if this isn't possible, make sure that the rack is tidy, the shoes are not dirty and they are arranged neatly in pairs.

Step Six – Decoration and Ornaments

What items does your child keep around their bed? Many children like to have their teddies around them and these are fine, provided they are not stacked up high, preventing good airflow when they sleep. Any sharp-edged and/or "high-energy" toys or teddies around your child should be put away when it's time to go to sleep.

If your child is anxious or has trouble sleeping, place lovely family photos or photos of their pets around their bed. Having these nearby will give them a feeling of love and security that they can draw comfort from.

What colour are the bedroom walls? Are they fiery colours like pinks, reds, purples, oranges or bright yellows? These can promote anxiety and stress, as they can overstimulate the senses by inducing a feeling of high energy. On the other hand, if the room is too muted and features colours like dark blues and greys, that can encourage a sense of low mood. You want to use warm (but not dull) colours, such as pastel shades. This is especially important for neurodiverse children because the brighter colours can be overstimulating.

I recently had a message from a lady called Lucia to say that she had just found me on Instagram but the week before she had painted her little boy's room in a Spiderman theme. Two walls were bright red and two walls deep blue – the boy loved it of course, but she was so worried about it. My advice in such situations is: if it's not broken, don't fix it. What I mean by that is, if your child sleeps fine and is as calm as a five-year-old should be, leave things as they are. But if they are struggling, try to find a way of calming the colours down a little.

In this digital age full of gadgets, phones and computers, it's surprising how many children still love having a television in their bedroom. I'm about to show my age, but I remember having a portable black-and-white TV in my own room – it even had an aerial. I thought all my Christmases had come at once! But in Feng Shui, televisions (especially in the bedroom) are seen as a no-no because of the energy they hold. They are also a huge distraction, so if your child really wants one, you could turn it off at the plug at night or even cover it with a towel or scarf to hold in some of that energy.

What artwork does your child have on their walls? For example, do they have brightly coloured posters featuring high-energy characters staring down at them while they are in bed? This could really impact their ability to sleep because these can be so stimulating as they are designed to get our attention. Maybe try to balance out anything like this with something less stimulating.

If your child is struggling with making friends, I would suggest having a picture of a group of people having fun together rather than photos or illustrations of just one single person, animal or item and so on.

One of the best things to do to help you assess your child's bedroom is to go and lie on your child's bed and have a good look around with a fresh pair of eyes. How does it make you feel? If you slept in that room, would you feel calm in it? If you feel calm, then your child is likely to feel calm too. If you lay on that bed and thought *"Oh my goodness! There is so much going on in this bedroom"*, then perhaps that is how your child is also feeling on the inside. The problem is that little ones don't have the ability to work this out for themselves, so we constantly have to guess and do it for them. Who said parenting is easy?

Step Seven – Mirrors

Mirrors are one of the things people ask me about all the time when it comes to Feng Shui. They're super powerful tools for so many reasons, like making a room feel bigger and brighter by reflecting light and giving the illusion of more space. However, they are also capable of speeding up the energy in a room, which can leave it feeling chaotic rather than calm. When it comes to children's bedrooms, there are a couple of places you really want to avoid putting a mirror.

First, try to avoid having a mirror directly opposite the child's bed because the energy will be bouncing right off the mirror and straight onto them, which can impact their sleep. And second, having a mirror that faces the window is not ideal either because it reflects the good energy right back out of the window – we want the good energy to stay and the bad energy to go. Another little tip is that if you've got mirrors facing each other, like those ones in changing rooms that allow you to see the back of your body (the ones I hate!), it's a good idea to move one of them. This is particularly relevant if your child is feeling anxious, as having two mirrors can double the energy, and if they're already stressed, it might be making them feel worse. If you can't take one down, even covering one with a scarf can help.

Step Eight – Lighting

Every morning, make it a habit to open the drapes or blinds in your child's room, as this is where all the good energy flows in! If you can, open the window for a while too, even if it's only for a short time. Letting some fresh air in works wonders for shifting the energy in the room. I do it every day, and it instantly makes the house feel fresher and more peaceful. Even in the winter in the UK, I used to open the window for at least 30 seconds. It's amazing how such a small thing can make such a big difference. Also, as mentioned previously, keep the windows clean! It might sound simple, but dirty windows block out some of that good energy. Clean windows let in bright, crisp sunlight, which brings a whole new feeling of vitality to the room.

Now, for the lighting. Does your child have a lamp by their bed? At bedtime, you want the light to be below eye level. This softer, lower light mimics sunset and sends a message to the brain that it's time to wind down. A warm-coloured lamp is perfect for creating that cosy, relaxing feeling. Definitely steer clear of harsh, bright white lights if you can. Think soft tones, not car showroom lights! If you've got a radio or a smart speaker, try playing some calming meditation music at bedtime. I always used to do this for my daughter when she was little, and it really helped to create a soothing, peaceful space for sleep. White noise is also amazing for children, especially if they find it difficult to calm their mind at nighttime.

Step Nine – Good Habits

When children come home from school, all too often a "pile of doom" of discarded clothes appears on the floor (often referred to as the "floordrobe"). Try to get them to hang up their clothes, although, to be honest, sometimes it's easier to do it yourself and avoid the United Nations negotiations! School uniforms carry all the energy from the day, so it's important to get them tidied up and/or put away. If your child has a laundry bin in their room, make sure it has a lid. That way, you can contain the energy from those clothes, whether it was a good day or a not-so-great one. You don't want it just hanging around and making the room feel off-balance.

Another good habit is to get your child to make their bed in the morning. Even if their efforts aren't quite up to your standards! There's a reason for doing this: when the bed is made, it helps set the tone for the day. It sends the signal to their brain that, "OK, the bed's made, you're not getting back into it!" I'm really big on this routine, even though my husband thinks I'm crazy for putting all the cushions back when we just take them off again at night! But it makes the room feel calm and put-together, and children feel that too, even if they don't consciously realize it. Being in a tidy room first thing in the morning can have a big influence on how they feel throughout the day.

Step Ten – Remedies and Extras

If your child is really struggling, you could cleanse their bedroom with sage. It may be best to do it when they aren't there, or you could get them involved. Make sure that the windows are open when you smoulder the sage. You do this by lighting the end of the sage and blow out the flame so it's smoking like an incense stick. You then work your way around their room and into the corners, so that the sage can burn off the negativity in all of the energy spots.

I also love to place an amethyst crystal in children's bedrooms as it is amazing for balancing emotions and therefore brings a sense of calm. It's also great for concentration, making it perfect if they are doing their homework in their room.

For children who are easily stimulated, you can create a little den or soft space in their bedroom by adding a bean bag or soft seating. Having a cosy, soft spot to sit is like a little retreat for them, a comfy place where they can relax and unwind. Whether it's a bean bag chair or a fluffy cushion in the corner, it gives children a space to decompress when they need a break from everything. It's their own little chill-out zone.

Finally, if you have space, add a plant that has soft green leaves in your child's room because this can bring a calming, natural energy to the room without being overwhelming.

I'm sure you're already doing a lot of what I've talked about here, but one of the biggest things to remember is to look at your child's room with fresh eyes. Children can't or won't always help themselves when it comes to their space, so it's up to us to guide them with what we know.

I truly believe that if you get children involved in these Feng Shui principles, like I do with my daughter, they'll start feeling the benefits themselves. Just gently explain what you're doing and why and encourage them to pick up these positive habits. It helps them understand what makes their room feel calm and relaxing, and they'll catch on quicker than you think. Feng Shui isn't just for adults, it's for everyone, including children.

Calming Children's Bedroom Checklist

Decluttering and Deep Cleaning

☑ Remove unused or unnecessary items to create a calm, clutter-free space

☑ Dust, vacuum and clean surfaces to refresh the energy in the room

Positioning Beds and Choosing Bedding Colours

☑ Put the bed in a commanding position, avoiding direct alignment with the door and ensuring a solid wall behind for support

☑ Choose soft, calming colours for bedding that promote rest and relaxation, avoiding overly bright or chaotic patterns

Managing Storage and the Bedside Area

☑ Ensure the space around the bed is open and uncluttered.

☑ Place reassuring family photos nearby for a sense of comfort and security

Placing Mirrors and Lighting, and Tidiness

☑ Avoid placing mirrors directly facing the bed, as this can be disruptive to sleep

☑ Use soft, warm lighting for a cosy atmosphere and ensure natural light flows into the room during the day

☑ Establish a daily habit of returning toys, books and clothes to their designated spots to maintain order

CHAPTER 9

BEAUTIFUL BATHROOMS

Cleansing and Flow

The bathroom can be one of the most overlooked spaces in the home when it comes to Feng Shui, yet it plays a crucial role in the energy of your space. If you think about it, this is where you cleanse, refresh and prepare yourself for the day ahead or unwind before bed. Water, which symbolizes wealth and energy flow in Feng Shui, is constantly moving in and out of this space. Without some simple Feng Shui tweaks, this can lead to energy being drained away, rather than nourishing the rest of your home. In this chapter, we'll explore how to optimize your bathroom using Feng Shui principles, from the ideal placement of key elements to small changes that make a big impact.

Supporting Positive Energy

You may have heard of one of the most common Feng Shui "rules" and that is always to close the toilet seat lid. This is because the bathroom is seen as a "waste room" in Feng Shui, so we do all we can to stop the good energy escaping from here. Toilets are literally seen as a drain in the home – both in the literal sense but also a drain on energy as well. As the energy enters, it flows beautifully around to give life to all the areas, bringing calm and happiness with it, but then it reaches the toilet, which takes this lovely energy and sucks it down the drain. This is why it's so important that we keep the toilet seat lid closed, because this will help to keep this positive energy in your home. I know that it might take some training of other members of your household, but I promise it's worth it. Make sure that you close the bathroom door as well, just to make it extra hard for the good energy to escape.

Cleanliness and Decluttering

If you listen to my podcast, you will know that I love the phrase "hotel pristine clean" because I feel it describes the level of cleanliness we need to achieve, which is far more than just a quick wipe down! If you want good energy to flow around your home, then I'm afraid that cleanliness (both in the normal meaning of the word and energetically as well) is absolutely essential. Bathrooms can be places where energy gathers because the whole point of the shower or bath is to cleanse and renew, so it can retain some of the energy we are cleansing from our minds and bodies. The last thing we want is for this energy to get stuck, and so regularly cleaning all surfaces, and mirrors in particular, will help because these reflect the energy around the room. Toothpaste splatters will just get in the way of the flow of good energy!

Don't forget to clean the drains as well, because blocked drains are said to represent blocked emotions. Also check the taps and showers for dripping water because that symbolizes opportunities and money slipping away. Funny how I don't mind cleaning the bathroom now that I know it can prevent money going down the drain – I used to hate it!

The power of decluttering the bathroom should not be underestimated either. Let's be honest, most bathrooms are small yet packed with half-empty bottles, expired products, and things like that hand cream you were given last Christmas. I'm terrible at wanting to keep things "for best" – I found a Jo Malone shower gel in the cupboard when we moved that I received about two years earlier and never got around to using! So first, you absolutely deserve to use that lovely shower gel every single day; and second, it's time to get everything – and I mean everything – out of the drawers and cupboards and go through them one by one. Most beauty products have a use-by date of a year, and I know I have some make-up that is much older than that. Throw away what you can't use and donate anything new that can be used by someone else. There are some wonderful charities who specifically collect toiletries, so such items will be gratefully received, I am sure.

Once you have decided what to keep, use some storage solutions to maximize the space. Things like medicine boxes, and drawer and cupboard organizers are great, especially if you are tight on space.

Decluttering isn't just about tidying up, it's about creating a beautiful space that feels calm and brings you happiness.

I also want to mention bins here. If you do have a bin in the bathroom, empty it often and make sure that it has a lid. My biggest revelation is having a recycling bin in my bathroom now, so I don't have to try to rescue soggy toilet rolls anymore!

The Power of Plants

Adding plants is a lovely way of introducing some positive energy to your bathroom – they don't just look attractive, they also do a great job of cleaning and purifying the area around them. Plants are part of the Wood element, so they bring a lovely growth energy but also an energy that helps with renewal, which is exactly what the bathroom is for.

Bathrooms obviously contain a lot of Water energy, which welcomes "flow" into your life so that things come and go. However, too much flow means that opportunities or money may come into your home, but literally fly out of the door as soon as they come in. We can use plants to balance this energy as the Wood element stabilizes and grounds the Water energy, creating an atmosphere that feels a lot calmer and more balanced. The bathroom isn't an easy environment for plants to thrive in, though, so choose ones that are happy being in lower-lit and humid areas. Bamboo is perfect because it still grows in these conditions, but also because it is known to attract luck and prosperity in Feng Shui. Ferns are lovely too, as they are soft and bring a tropical feeling to the bathroom, but they are also great at filtering the air around them.

Try to avoid spiky plants like cacti because they give off a piercing energy, and also plants that have trailing vines because we are looking for a growth energy that is strong and supportive.

Bathroom Décor

Mirrors in the bathroom are obviously pretty essential but try to be mindful about where you place them. If you can, put them where they don't directly reflect the toilet or shower because that can double up the "waste" energy.

Using the correct colours in the bathroom can balance the energy in the space and this will help to create a feeling of calm and relaxation. As the bathroom is associated with Water, we need to add colours that will complement this element, and slow some of this energy down so that wealth and opportunities stay. The first thing is to indicate what colours to avoid or use sparingly, and that would be more of the Water element colours: anything from the lightest blues you see in the Maldives to the rich dark blues and blacks found in the deeper seas in the Atlantic, for example. The bathroom is already dominated by the Water element due to its connection to sinks, showers, toilets and drains. Adding more blue – especially deep blues and blacks – can overwhelm the space with too much Water energy, creating an unbalanced environment. This can lead to feelings of stagnation, emotional instability or a sense that opportunities and money are constantly "draining away".

One lady I worked with had just decorated her whole bathroom in a lovely navy blue with lots of water-themed pictures. Although it looked beautiful, she said that anything that could have gone wrong with the decoration process did – it cost far more than she was expecting, and it just felt draining from start to finish. If you also have blue bathrooms and your home feels draining and money isn't staying, please don't worry as you can add some of the colours below through the décor or towels.

Greens are wonderful for the bathroom because they are associated with the Wood element. It goes so well with the Water element, as it helps to calm it without destroying the energy. Sage greens, pine, olive, pistachio or seaweed colours are perfect. Whites and neutrals are also good because they symbolize cleanliness and are lovely and light, great for smaller bathrooms or ones with few windows. Ivory, beige or even soft grey bring a sense of calm to the room as well, without disrupting the Water energy too much. Earthy tones are great because they help to stabilize Water. Sandy beiges or taupes also work really well and are still bright enough for smaller bathrooms.

Your bathroom doesn't have to be bland though. You can introduce some pastel shades as well, like blush pinks or pale peaches, as this will help to lift the energy in the room. We also still need a bit of Yang energy in the bathroom. Natural materials are perfect from a Feng Shui point of view, just because they are natural: wooden features and stone tiles are very effective for balancing the energy.

Natural scents keep the bathroom fresh. I often add a couple of drops of essential oils into the plug hole or on a cotton wool ball and it makes the room smell so nice, without overloading on chemical smells.

Finally, I wouldn't recommend having family photos in the bathroom, because you are surrounding them with "waste" energy and you don't want them "looking" at you while you are in there either! Instead, choose some calming images that help to bring a feeling of relaxation to the room.

The Bathroom Pièce de Résistance

I'm now going to ask you to tie some red ribbon around the pipes under your sink. I know this sounds utterly bonkers, but in Feng Shui, tying red ribbon around pipes is like putting a little protective seal on your energy flow, especially when it comes to money. You can do this on as many pipes around the home as you like, and it's all about symbolically stopping your wealth from draining away. I am sure there are many plumbers around the world who are wondering what on earth is going on!

Incorporating these Feng Shui principles into your bathroom can create a space that feels calm, balanced and rejuvenating. By focusing on such small but meaningful adjustments, your bathroom can become more than a functional space, and transform into a serene retreat that supports relaxation and well-being – and may even boost your bank balance too!

Beautiful Bathrooms Checklist

Decluttering and Organizing

- ☑ Remove expired products, half-used bottles and unnecessary items
- ☑ Use storage solutions to keep things tidy

Cleaning Regularly

- ☑ Aim for a "hotel pristine clean" standard.
- ☑ Pay special attention to mirrors, drains, and taps to ensure energy flows freely

Positioning the Toilet Lid and the Door

- ☑ Prevent good energy from being drained away by keeping the toilet lid down
- ☑ Close the bathroom door

Choosing Décor and Artwork, and Positioning Mirrors

- ☑ Avoid excessive use of blue and blacks.
- ☑ Use décor elements in green, earthy tones and soft neutrals to stabilize the Water-dominated space.
- ☑ Opt for calming images instead of Water-themed pictures or family photos
- ☑ Ensure mirrors don't directly reflect the toilet or shower to prevent doubling the "waste" energy

Selecting Plants and Natural Elements

- ☑ Introduce greenery like bamboo or ferns to purify the air and stabilize energy flow, and avoid spiky or trailing plants
- ☑ Use wood and stone materials and natural scents to bring warmth and balance

Managing Bins and Pipes

- ☑ Keep a lidded bin (and even a small recycling bin) and empty it regularly
- ☑ Symbolically prevent wealth from "draining away" with the simple Feng Shui remedy of tying a red ribbon around them.

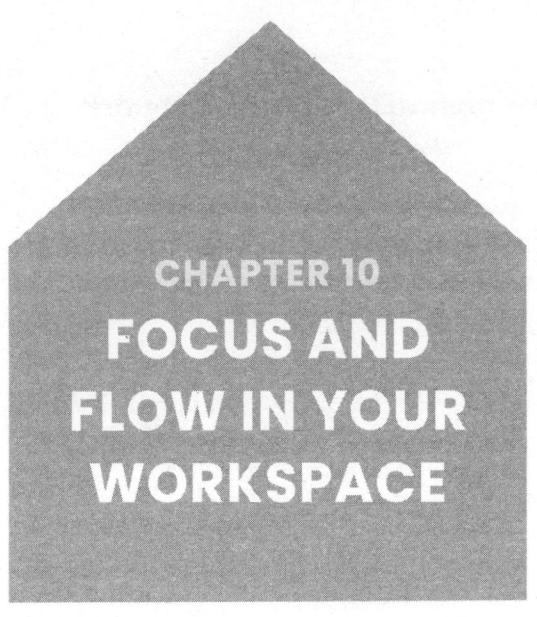

CHAPTER 10
FOCUS AND FLOW IN YOUR WORKSPACE

Many of us now find ourselves working from home at least for some of the week, if not most or all of the time. For many, the home "office" is the dining room table or perhaps a temporary desk in the bedroom; or you may have your own proper office at home, which is amazing. Wherever you work in your home, there are some things you can do to help concentration and efficiency, reduce stress and help you to attract more success into your life.

Amanda Hawes shared her top tips for designing work or study spaces for neurodivergent family members, and it involved two main ideas: minimizing distractions and incorporating sensory-friendly elements.

"For individuals with ADHD (attention deficit hyperactivity disorder), a clutter-free desk, noise-cancelling headphones, fidget items and visual timers can enhance focus. For those with autism, sensory tools like fidget items or weighted lap pads can provide comfort.

Remember that with fidget items not all fidgets are made equal ... some are perfect for focus, while others are used for distraction. Identifying the best ones for the right purpose is important.

Research details the importance of personalization of an environment, such as allowing individuals to choose colours or decorations that inspire and motivate them, enhance their sense of calmness and control and allow focus and creativity to flow. The inclusion of natural light and comfortable ergonomic furniture, such as desk chair, desk height and screen height, can further support concentration and engagement, promoting task completion and productivity, as well as boosting well-being."

Desk Position

The most important thing to think about is the position of your desk, because this really can help or hinder your productivity and the feeling of empowerment. Ideally, you want your desk to be in the "command position", which means that you can see the door, but without being directly in front of it. Sitting in this position symbolizes being in control and being able to see what's coming both physically and metaphorically. The ability to see the door will help you feel less drained and bring fewer surprises your way.

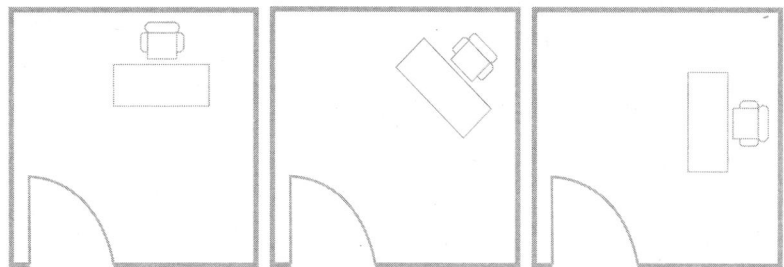

Figure 15. Examples of the desk being in the "command position"

You also want to sit with your back against the wall, rather than the door or the window – and I know that most offices are designed to have the desk against the wall with the seat facing it. From a Feng Shui perspective, this really doesn't help because it may make you feel vulnerable and unsupported. When your back faces an open space, it's harder to feel secure, which can impact your ability to concentrate.

If you aren't able to change your desk position, though, don't worry as you can add a small mirror or a mirrored photo frame to your desk to reflect the door. This may sound simple, but it means that you are still able to see what or who is coming, which will relax you and enable you to focus more easily.

If your desk must face the wall, you can create a sense of support by adding a plant, a piece of furniture or a strong piece of artwork behind you. Personally, I love pictures of herds of elephants in workspaces – they symbolize strength, teamwork and protection, all of which are essential for success in your job or business.

At the same time, try to avoid positioning your desk with your back to the door or a window. This setup can create feelings of vulnerability and instability, making it harder to concentrate and take confident decisions. When your back is exposed to open space, you may subconsciously feel unprotected, which can affect focus and productivity. Instead, aim for a setup where you have a clear view of the room, reinforcing a sense of security and control.

A Cluttered Space Means a Cluttered Mind

If you are a procrastinator, struggle to concentrate, or lack clarity and creativity, then your workspace could be to blame. When your desk is full of paper, random items and coffee cups, it can bring a chaotic energy to your work environment. This can feel draining, and it will be much harder to concentrate because the energy will get stuck. Remember, the more stuff that is in the way, the harder it is for energy to circulate.

Keep essentials on your desk and sort through paperwork at the end of every day. Seeing piles of paper can resemble a huge "to-do" list, which is exhausting. This goes for your computer as well. Make sure that you have a really good filing system set up so that everything has a home and your desktop is completely clear of random files.

Clearing your desk at the end of the day is very powerful, especially if you have had a terrible day. It's like hitting the control-alt-delete buttons – it resets everything. Every day should be a clean slate with opportunities to welcome something new and exciting into your life. I also use an energetic cleansing spray that helps to clear the energy every day too. You can buy them online or, if you are feeling creative, you can make one yourself – see instructions below. I call this one "Clear Vibe" because it cleanses negative energy and raises vibrations.

Clear Vibe Spray

You will need:

- ◆ **Spray bottle**
- ◆ **Distilled water**
- ◆ **Witch-hazel**
- ◆ **Pinch of sea salt**
- ◆ **10 drops lavender essential oil** (for calm)
- ◆ **10 drops lemon essential oil** (for positivity and concentration)
- ◆ **5 drops frankincense or sage essential oil** (for protection)
- ◆ **A crystal such as clear quartz to amplify the energy of the spray** (optional)

Simply add the ingredients to the bottle and shake. Then spray the mixture either where you work or on yourself!

Low-key Lighting

Natural light is one of the most powerful ways to boost productivity and bring more positive energy into your workspace. Research has shown that exposure to natural light in the workplace significantly enhances productivity (Boubekri et al, 2014)[1] . Natural light helps to regulate your circadian rhythm by telling your body that it's time to be awake. Office spaces with very little natural light will, over time, make you feel tired and you will have trouble concentrating. They don't help your mood either, so the more natural light you can get into a space, the better. Natural light also makes you feel that you are connected to the world outside of your work, and that there is more to life than what's happening on your computer.

If you don't have much access to natural light, there are ways to get around this, so don't worry. Artificial lighting has come a long way since the fluorescent tubes we used to have at home when growing up – I'm sure you could get a tan from those things! Soft lighting is perfect, and layering lighting with some overhead lights, desk lights and floor lamps will help to reduce shadows, which is important because these can lead to eye strain. If you do have overhead lighting, avoid sitting directly underneath it because energetically this can put pressure on you.

I love table lamps, especially if you can adjust the brightness, because this will help you to adjust the mood throughout the day. I know that sometimes I need the brightness, but at other times I like the room to feel darker and cosier. Lighting isn't only a practical feature, it's also a lovely way of making your working environment feel more comfortable and supportive.

Placing Mirrors and Plants

Mirrors need to be given a little bit of thought before you add them. They are great at making the room feel lighter and brighter, but they are also capable of reflecting and amplifying whatever energy is surrounding them. If you are facing a mirror when you work, it won't only mirror your physical appearance, but also perhaps any stress and chaos around you. So, if your work makes you feel overwhelmed and you can see yourself in a mirror, it could double up those feelings.

Adding plants around where you work is one of the best ways to bring in more good energy. Plants are associated with the Wood element and this represents growth, strength and vitality. They are very good for uplifting the energy of the space, as well as bringing a sense of fresh and new energy. If you lack creativity, including plants in your workspace is a really simple way to help with this. They also help to purify the air by absorbing toxins and releasing fresh new oxygen. This is great if you spend long hours at your desk, because it's going to support both your physical and mental well-being. This is why it blows my mind that so many larger offices have artificial plants that don't bring anything positive to the space around them – they simply gather dust and bring a stagnant energy to the area.

When choosing plants, make sure you go for ones that are easy to look after and have soft green leaves that grow upward, rather than downward. The Areca palm is a good choice because it has lovely soft leaves with a gracious flow to them that helps soften the energy. They are also amazing at absorbing toxins around them and studies have proved that:

"Indoor plants improve air quality by absorbing toxins through their leaves and roots, effectively reducing pollutants such as benzene,

*formaldehyde, and trichloroethylene." NASA Clean Air Study
(Wolverton et al., 1989)*

Adding Personal Touches

You can add some personal touches to your desk space, like a photo, some crystals, if you like. I love to have an amethyst on my desk because it is known to help with stress, anxiety, anger and any heightened emotions. It is also believed to help with mental clarity, focus and decision-making, so if you struggle with mental blockages it can help. Amethyst is also a protective stone as well; it can ward off negativity both from people but also from Electromagnetic Fields (EMFs). These are areas of energy that are produced by electrically charged objects. EMFs are generated by both natural sources (like the Earth's magnetic field) and human-made sources (like power lines, Wi-Fi routers and mobile phones). So, amethysts are an amazing crystal to have on your desk.

If you feel that you are surrounded by technology, you could add a grounding mat underneath your desk. The idea behind these is based on the concept of earthing, which suggests that direct contact with the Earth's electrons can help reduce inflammation, improve sleep and balance the body's electrical charge. The mats are designed to help neutralize the free radicals that we might be surrounded by. But if you aren't able to do this, tourmaline crystals are great at helping to absorb electromagnetic energy.

Setting Your Intentions

Feng Shui is powered by the intentions we put into everything we do, and the workspace is no different. It will reflect the energy of the person using the space, so how you feel when you are in that space can either help or hinder your goals and aspirations. Take a moment and think about an intention you want for yourself. For example, is it more wealth, creativity or balance?

Once you have your intentions, consider if your workspace reflects them. If you are looking for more wealth, do you have visual affirmations of what wealth means to you around you? A super, simple way of doing this is to change your screensaver to something that you want to attract into your life. Are you looking for more creativity? If so, is your desk area dull and boring, or does it feel bright and light, allowing you to think more creatively? If you want more balance, does your workspace feel calm or is it a little chaotic? And so on.

I find that having intentions helps me get through the harder days too, as it gives me purpose and grit on the days when I need it. But make sure that you keep updating your intentions. I had a screensaver of Bondi Beach for about a year before we moved from the UK, and I got so used to seeing it that it was still there about six months after we moved here. It's amazing how we get used to what we are surrounded by, so even if you need to set a calendar reminder, remember to keep updating your visions regularly

Finally, if you work from the dining room or your bedroom, make sure that you put everything away at the end of the day, in either a drawer or a box with a lid on it to keep the energy contained. Otherwise, it will feel like you are living in your office, and you won't ever feel you can escape from work.

Incorporating Feng Shui into your workspace covers much more than just how it looks. For example, creating a space that feels balanced helps you think more clearly and be more productive in your daily life. When your workspace flows harmoniously, so does your work, allowing you to feel more inspired, efficient and less stressed throughout your day.

Focus and Flow in Your Workspace Checklist

Positioning and Setting up Your Desk

- ☑ Place your desk in the command position – facing the room with a clear view of the door (not directly in front of it).
- ☑ Avoid sitting with your back to the door or window. If unavoidable, use a mirror to reflect the door
- ☑ If facing a wall, add a plant, artwork or furniture behind you for support

Decluttering and Organization

- ☑ Keep your desk clear of clutter – only essentials should remain
- ☑ Store paperwork neatly and clear your desk daily to reset the energy
- ☑ Organize digital files – keep your desktop tidy for mental clarity

Cleansing and Enhancing Energy

- ☑ Use an energetic cleansing spray daily
- ☑ Add a small crystals like amethyst (for focus) or tourmaline (for EMF protection)
- ☑ Incorporate plants to improve air quality and create positive energy

Creating Desired Lighting and Atmosphere

☑ Maximize natural light – keep windows clear and open when possible

☑ Layer artificial lighting (desk lamps, floor lamps) for a balanced environment

☑ Avoid sitting directly under overhead lights to reduce energetic pressure

Personalizing Your Space and Intentions

☑ Set clear intentions for your workspace – focus, success, creativity and so on

☑ Use visual affirmations (screensavers, artwork) that reflect your goals

☑ Update your workspace regularly to keep the energy fresh and inspiring

Setting up a Temporary Office (Bedroom/Dining Room)

☑ Store work items in a box with a lid at the end of the day to contain energy

☑ Ensure your space transitions from work to relaxation effectively

CHAPTER 11

RESTFUL AND ROMANTIC BEDROOMS

Feng Shui in the bedroom can make a big difference when it comes to creating a space that helps you relax and feel connected. By arranging your bedroom in a way that encourages good energy flow, you can create a space that encourages better sleep and a stronger romantic vibe. This chapter explains how, with a few adjustments, your bedroom can become the perfect spot for both relaxation and romance.

Setting Intentions

As you know by now, Feng Shui isn't the same as manifestation. While manifestation focuses on thoughts and intentions, Feng Shui is far more powerful because it actively works with the energy in your home to create real shifts in all areas of your life. When it comes to love and romance, the energy in your space plays a significant role in your relationships, whether you are calling in a new partner, healing from a past relationship, or seeking to reignite passion in an existing one.

If you feel the energy from a previous relationship lingers, clearing that is essential to make way for fresh, loving energy to enter. Or if you are in a relationship at the moment, your home can have a huge impact on either helping or hindering your connection. This chapter outlines all the things you can do to bring warmth and intimacy back, while also creating a space in your home where you can rest.

I get a lot of questions from people when they are having difficulties in certain areas of their lives, and a really common topic is love and romance – whether they are in a relationship with a partner they already live with and the quality of their love life needs to improve, or they are wanting to attract a new partner. I believe it's a really important subject because we all want love and romance in our lives, and there are definitely things that you can do in your home to improve this.

The first thing is to think about what you actually want. At the beginning of the book, I spoke about Feng Shui being the missing part of the manifestation puzzle and this is about being *really clear* about your intentions. However, with relationships, this isn't always easy to do, so please do take your time to think about it.

I worked with a lovely client, Samira, who was from the UK, and she kept attracting the same type of person into her life over and over again. She was in a cycle of one bad guy after the next, so I asked her what her intentions were when it came to finding a partner. Her response was "I just want to be in a relationship". So here is Rule 1 of setting your intentions to attract a partner: be SUPER clear. You don't want just anyone in your life. Think of the characteristics you want them to have – someone kind, who loves you for who you are, who is funny and who you are attracted to. Try saying this affirmation and writing it on sticky notes to put around the home in places where you'll see it frequently: "I am ready to attract the right partner into my life."

If you're looking for a partner, ensure that your home has physical space for them. Do you have room at the table? Is there space in your bed? One of my clients from the USA, Maria, was single and hoping to attract a partner. When I was sent photos of her apartment, I noticed that while she had a beautiful balcony, there was only one chair – symbolically leaving no space for someone else. Simply by adding another chair, she created room for a partner in her life.

Beyond physical space, it's important to make energetic space as well. This means ensuring you have time in your schedule to welcome and nurture a relationship. Think of it as starting a new chapter of love and romance. What has happened up until today has been and gone – it's time to look forward and change the energy in your life and your home.

Next, I recommend that you write down what or who it is that you are wanting to attract into your life. What are your intentions and affirmations? Writing them down can be so powerful because it helps you to believe that they really can come true. Here are some that you could use for attracting a new partner:

- ◆ I welcome more love into my life
- ◆ I deserve to be in a happy and fulfilled relationship
- ◆ I love myself and am open to love
- ◆ The more love I give, the more I receive
- ◆ I deserve to be loved just the way I am

And here are some examples of affirmations you could use if you are already in a relationship, and you wish to enhance it:

- ◆ **Our love grows stronger and deeper every day**
- ◆ **Our physical and emotional bond grows stronger every day**
- ◆ **We communicate openly, honestly and with love**
- ◆ **We make time for romance and nurture our relationship daily**
- ◆ **Our relationship is filled with joy, laughter and mutual respect.**

I recommend that you keep these in the Southwest area of your home, but if that room belongs to someone else, then place these in your bedroom. You can fold them up and hide them away or you can even put them under your crystals to add more energy to them, because the crystals can give your affirmations superpowers.

Making Things Happen

First, you want to clear any negative energy in the home, which you will be well on your way to doing if you have started to declutter. But for love and romance, there is another layer to the decluttering process – although I promise you will still have some items left in your home by the time you have finished this book!

The first thing that I'm going to ask you to do is have a look around your home. And when I say that I also mean the loft, bedside cabinets, drawers, literally everywhere. You're going to be looking for anything that holds any negative emotions associated with relationships, both current and past. It might be photos, it might be letters, it might even be places that you've visited, and you still have travel tickets from there that you're holding on to. The importance of the decluttering process becomes really clear and hopefully a little easier when you realize the impact these items have on all areas of your life. Any items that trigger feelings of insecurity, sadness or just attracting the wrong person need to go!

Do you have items in your wardrobe that make you feel sad when you see them? You may have worn them on a date that was awful, or at a time in your relationship that wasn't good at all. Take these items out and have a think about whether or not you are able to change how you feel when you see them. If not, send them on to have a new life with someone else. This also includes your wedding clothes if you have separated from your partner.

One client, Hana, was looking for a new relationship and when she was going through the decluttering process, she realized that she still had her wedding dress in her wardrobe in her bedroom, and her bedroom colour theme was purple (I will explain this later in the chapter, but let's just say it wasn't helping matters.). Keeping a wedding dress from a previous relationship really isn't going to help you move on to the next chapter. However, if you *really* want to keep it because you genuinely believe you will pass it on to someone else, then have it cleaned and boxed and put it in the attic – or anywhere apart from your bedroom or the Southwest of your home.

An article of clothing that holds negative energy for you doesn't have to be as significant as a wedding dress. It could be an outfit that you've worn on dates or something that you've taken on vacation. It could be something that you've bought while on vacation when you've been in a relationship before. Or if it's the same relationship that you're in now, but you've had unhappy times where you don't feel secure and happy and loved, then it's still time for it to move on. It might be something that you have purchased at a time when you weren't that happy.

I had a client who had a picture she bought on vacation when she was going through a really difficult time in her marriage, and she had this in the entrance of her home. It hadn't even crossed her mind before, but every time she entered her home, she saw this picture and it made her sad – so you can see how items in your home may look energetically innocent, but they could be having a big impact on your day-to-day life. Removing these items from your home will allow you to breathe a little bit and not be filled with this constant feeling of negativity about your current or previous relationships. The idea is that you are trying to welcome in energy filled with love and romance, so you don't want to be held back by any tricky energy surrounding items in your home.

Really dig deep around your home because it's crazy what you can find. I was having this conversation with somebody a few months ago and she said: "I've got a picture of my first ever boyfriend upstairs in the loft, just in case my daughter ever wanted to see it." And I get that. But just because it's in the loft doesn't mean that its energy isn't filtering into your home, especially as lofts are often directly above where we sleep. This energy can seep down into our bedrooms, and that's not what we want. So, once you have got out all those clothes, photos, tickets and so on that cause negative memories, and then got rid of them, you need to cleanse your home. It's a bit like a beauty regime – there's more than one step!

Every time you go through items, you are unblocking stagnant energy that has been sitting there for a long time. You are then taking it through your home and leaving a trail of this energy. Make sure that the windows are open in the room you are sorting, and then afterwards, open the doors. You can also smudge your home with sage (see page 122) or just walk through with an incense stick or candle to burn off this energy. Obviously, be careful with sage and candles if you're moving them around your home but open those windows and let that energy go. When you have done this, take a moment to really feel the energetic shift, because when you feel it, your vibration and your own energy change, and that is exactly what you want, to either attract somebody new or improve the relationship that you currently have.

If you want to take clearing out the old energy one step further – and this isn't for everybody, I know – you could even write down your feelings. Express exactly how you felt before – how angry, upset or even betrayed – and then take this piece of paper outside and burn it. It's almost like you're burning through those thoughts and the things that have happened, and therefore they no longer exist. That part of life is done, it's over and you are ready to welcome in something new. Again, please be careful if you are setting fire to things in your garden. I can confirm that my neighbour must think I'm bonkers because they hear me opening my door, welcoming the good energy, opening the back door, getting rid of the bad energy and randomly setting fire to pieces of paper in our garden! I think I've just got to the point where I own it now. I am out, I am loud and I am proud to be the Feng Shui consultant that I am!

Artwork for Love and Romance

I'd like you to look around your home and consider the pictures or artwork you have. From a love and romance perspective, we want to promote the feeling of being in a couple and so should avoid any pictures of solitary people, animals and objects, as they symbolize the feeling and energy of doing life alone. We want to promote the energy of being with someone, while also promoting equality in the relationship.

I remember working with a client who, at the entrance of her home, had a poster that said, "Alone by herself, she built the kingdom she wanted". She had worked so hard to build her life and have an amazing home, but now she wanted to enjoy her life with someone else. I asked her to think about how someone would feel coming into her home and seeing that poster. Would they feel welcome? I'm not saying that she shouldn't have been proud about what she had achieved – absolutely, she should be. But it was now time for a new chapter, and moving this picture was a really important sign that she was emotionally ready to share her world with someone new.

The Southwest and Your Bedroom: Two Key Spaces

We're now going to look specifically at the Southwest of your home, because if you remember, this area looks after your love life and relationships. Sometimes, this isn't the most ideal part. For example, it might house your teenager's bedroom or your bathroom, but wherever it is, don't panic. There is also a bonus area in your home for love and romance, and that is your bedroom.

I would place anything in these areas (both the Southwest and your bedroom) that reminds you of what you want to attract. Whether it's in your current relationship or a new relationship, I find visual tools such as photos and pictures really helpful. I call these *visual affirmations* because when you look at them, they have the power to change your energy and the energy around them, and that is exactly what we are trying to do. Have pictures or photos of anything that feels romantic or full of love that is supportive of you and gives off a vibe of security. It could be a picture of two people out for dinner, walking or just sitting in the garden together. The most important thing is that the picture has two people in it and not just one. If you don't have a picture of you and your partner, you can buy a beautiful postcard or a greetings card. You could also have ornaments of couples together or of hearts. But make sure that you feature two hearts and not just one, because you don't want to have one heart in the relationship.

The other thing that you can do is keep some crystals in the bedroom. I give examples of these in chapter 6: Crystals and Feng Shui.

The main point of these tasks is to create an energy that is fueled by love and romance in the Southwest of your home and in your bedroom.

Choosing Colours for the Bedroom

I'd like you to think about the colours in your bedroom. Do they represent a flow of calm, loving energy? If you have too many fiery colours in this area, such as reds, pinks, oranges, yellows and so on, this could bring a burning energy to your relationship, and we absolutely don't want that. As I mentioned earlier, purple is to be avoided too, as this colour has a reputation of bringing sexual frustration to the bedroom! Aim for neutrals, just like a hotel room, or greens as these represent the Wood Element, or earthy tones because they will help to bring a lovely grounding feeling to the room.

Amanda Hawes believes that certain colours, textures and materials have a calming effect on neurodiverse individuals.

"Soft, muted colours like blues, greens and greys are often associated with relaxation and reduced anxiety, as supported by research in the environmental psychology field (Küller et al., 2009). It is also known that bright and busy patterns in a room such as on the wall with paints, wallpapers or prints, on the bedding, as well as intense and vivid colours like red or neon shades in wall hangings, can sometimes be overstimulating for neurodiverse people, particularly those with sensory sensitivities."

Positioning Your Bed

In Feng Shui, the position of your bed plays a crucial role in promoting restful sleep and harmonious relationships. According to Feng Shui, a solid headboard will give you a feeling of solidarity and help you to feel less anxious and ideally, it should be made from solid (not slatted) wood because it gives a feeling of security. The best placement is once again the "command position", which I have already explained in chapter 8: Children's Bedrooms.

Additionally, keeping the space beneath your bed clear is essential for maintaining a smooth and balanced energy flow. Storing clutter, old belongings or emotionally charged items under the bed can create stagnant energy, which may disrupt sleep and impact your well-being. For optimal Feng Shui to support a peaceful and loving atmosphere, ensure that the area under your bed remains open or is used only for soft, sleep-related items like extra bedding.

Your bedroom is more than a place to sleep; it is also at the heart of love and intimacy, and a place to recharge. By applying Feng Shui principles, you can create a space that nurtures connection, harmony and deep rest. A balanced bedroom invites love into your life, strengthens existing relationships and promotes emotional well-being. From decluttering to positioning your bed correctly and incorporating soothing colours and objects in pairs, every detail contributes to the energy flow in your space. When your bedroom reflects balance and intention, it becomes a sanctuary where love and relaxation can thrive, allowing you to wake up each day feeling refreshed, supported and aligned with your desires

It's as easy as that!

Restful and Romantic Bedroom Checklist

Setting Clear Intentions

☑ Define exactly what you want in a partner or a relationship
☑ Write down affirmations that align with your goals
☑ Ensure your home reflects the energy you want to attract
☑ Keep affirmations under crystals for extra energy

Making Space for Love

☑ Physically create space for a partner (have an extra chair, room in the bed and so on)
☑ Energetically clear space by letting go of past relationship baggage

Decluttering and Removing Negative Energy

☑ Get rid of items that hold emotional ties to past relationships

- ☑ Check your wardrobe, bedside tables, loft and even old tickets or photos
- ☑ Remove or store wedding clothes from previous marriages (but not in your bedroom or the Southwest of your home)
- ☑ Open windows and cleanse the space with sage, incense or candles

Enhancing the Love Energy

- ☑ Place romantic imagery/artwork in the Southwest area and bedroom (avoid solo images)
- ☑ Use items in pairs (for example – two hearts, two candles, two ornaments)
- ☑ Consider adding love-related crystals in key areas

Checking Bedroom Feng Shui

- ☑ Use calming, neutral or earthy tones (avoid fiery reds, pinks and purples)
- ☑ Ensure a solid headboard for stability in relationships
- ☑ Keep under-bed storage minimal and free of emotionally charged items
- ☑ Position the bed in a "command position" for better energy flow

Welcoming New Energy

- ☑ Write down and release old emotions (burning the paper as a symbolic reset)
- ☑ Maintain an open and inviting energy throughout the home

PART THREE

EMBRACE THE FENG SHUI LIFESTYLE

CHAPTER 12
MOVING HOME FASTER

Think of that lovely feeling when you walk into a hotel – the soft lighting, the uncluttered space, the gorgeous colours and textures. Your shoulders relax, your breath slows and you feel instantly at ease, as if all the stress of the outside world has melted away. That's exactly the feeling you want potential buyers and renters to experience the moment they step into your home.

Feng Shui helps create this emotional connection by helping good energy flow throughout the space. It starts at the entrance, where a clear, inviting doorway welcomes positive energy (and potential residents!) inside. The layout, colours and placement of furniture all play a role in ensuring energy moves freely, creating a sense of balance, warmth and security.

Decluttering and depersonalizing allow people to see themselves living in the space. You can add some small touches, such as fresh flowers, adjusting lighting or incorporating more earthy tones, because this will help give a feeling of stability and well-being, making the home feel like a sanctuary.

Whether you're selling or renting, Feng Shui ensures that your space not only looks appealing but also feels welcoming. After all, people don't just choose a house or an apartment, they choose *the feeling* of home.

Moving Starts with Shared Goals

Before you begin the process of moving, take a moment to reflect on whether or not you and everyone in your household are truly ready for this transition. If someone feels resistant to moving, that energy can create obstacles in the process. Open and honest conversations are so important to make sure that everyone is on board. By creating a sense of excitement and positivity about the move, you'll naturally create an uplifting energy within the home. This can help attract the right buyer or renter and make the process smoother and more successful.

If you have small children who are a little nervous about moving, you could ask them to draw their dream home or think of a list of things they would love to have in their new place. I know this could be a bit risky because when I was little, I wanted nothing more than a slide from my bedroom to downstairs! But hopefully there will be a couple of things you can realistically provide in the new place.

Moving can be difficult for adults too, and perhaps you yourself don't really want to go. If so, then I really recommend doing the cord-cutting exercise below.

The Cord-Cutting Exercise

Moving home can be a very emotional process, and this is totally understandable. Sometimes, it might be that you have such wonderful memories of your home that you don't want to leave; or it might be the opposite – that you have had a really hard time and there are lots of sad associations with it that you need to release.

Whichever emotions you are feeling, you can do what's called a cord-cutting exercise to help you detach yourself from your home. I have an audio on my website called "Letting Go" that will help you with this. But essentially, it is a visualization exercise where you see your home in front of you, attached by a physical cord, which will help you to make peace with those emotions. As mad as it may sound, it's also worth trying to have a conversation with your home and to thank it for looking after you by stating that it's time for you to all move on. I would also ask it to help you find a buyer (or a renter) – I did this before we moved to Australia. I thanked our house for looking after us for the last 14 years and told it that it was time for us to have a new adventure, but I'd really like its help to find a nice new family to live there. It was such a funny feeling because as soon as I said that, I didn't feel half as emotional about moving as I had done before.

Once you've had this conversation with your home (you can do this in your mind if you aren't comfortable saying it out loud), you can begin to visualize cutting through the physical cord between yourself and your home. If other people in your household don't want to move, they could try this exercise too. If they aren't quite ready to do this, you can at least have a conversation about what is making them hesitate to move on. This is an extremely powerful exercise, and it has helped so many people sell and rent out their homes because it literally shifts the energy.

Visualizing Your Future Home

Now it's time to think about where you are moving to. Do you have somewhere lined up? If there is any question or doubt about your future plans, it may make the move that little bit more difficult. I know a lot of people like to put their home up for sale or rent to "test the market", but I really recommend that you start the process of looking and viewing places. Or at the very least, write a wish-list outlining what you want in your new home.

Think about the location, appearance, how many bedrooms you need, the kitchen, and so on, as well as the price. The more detailed you can make it, the higher your energy will be in attracting somewhere that meets your requirements. You could also make a vision board, which is a sort of visual wish-list for your new place. You can cut out images of locations, ideal houses and apartments and colours you like from glossy magazines and pin them on a board or stick them on a piece of card. Display this somewhere you will see your vision board often, such as in the kitchen or hallway. Or you could make a digital version by downloading online images and making a collage of them on your computer – whatever works best for you. And don't forget to use affirmations (see page 39). The more positive energy you invest in the move, the sooner it will happen and the better it will be.

Decluttering (Again!)

I'm going to sound like a broken record now, but have you started taking action to move yet? If not, I really encourage you to begin by decluttering again as soon as possible. Go up into the loft and into the garage, and start the big clear-out. Only take with you the things that deserve to be in your new home, because this will bring good energy with you into your new place. By decluttering now, you are also putting the message out there that you are serious about moving, and your current home will feel so much lighter and better when people come round to view it. They need to see that your cupboards aren't bursting at the seams too, so that their belongings will fit easily into your home.

Committing to Selling or Renting

A big part of the home-selling or -renting process, which some people feel quite resistant to, is putting up a "For Sale" or "To Let" sign, if your local council allows it. If you don't have a sign, you are basically saying to the universe that you don't want to sell or rent out your home. You must be loud and proud about this, because you never know who is driving past on the off chance or checking out the neighbourhood, looking for a new place to settle in.

The next step is to set your intention of moving by printing off a copy of your particulars in big red letters with the amount you want to sell or rent it for right across the front, then writing SOLD or LET across it. Most importantly, add the date you want to sell or start renting it. Place this somewhere you will see it regularly – for example on your fridge – so that you get a positive feeling every time you see it. The whole point of each of these tasks is to improve the energy around selling or renting out your home.

The Galloping Horse

Finally, here's another slightly left-of-centre tip, which stems from a common theory used in Feng Shui. If you have ever stood near galloping horses – for example, at the races – you know the power they create, and this is what we are going to use to help sell or rent out your home.

Place a galloping black or brass horse statue (brass is better but slightly harder to get hold of) just inside your front door with its head facing the door as if it is galloping out through it. This symbolizes the energy moving out of the door, and you can even write something underneath it like "Thank you for helping us achieve a price that exceeds our expectations for our home and for helping us seamlessly move to our dream place".

If it's not possible to use a statue, you could use a greetings card or print off a picture of a galloping horse instead – it's not quite so powerful, that's all. One acquaintance of mine was trying to sell her apartment in Scotland and she lived in the south of the UK, so she sent a postcard of a galloping horse to her flat. Guess what, it worked!

In another example, Anne, a woman on my Practitioner course, said that when she was trying to move, it was considered the "worst time" for real estate because houses just weren't selling. So, she placed the horse statue inside her front door and they had the busiest Open Day the agent had had in a long time! And she sold her home for far more than the asking price.

As you prepare to move, remember that this process is about more than just transactions; it's about energy, flow and creating an inviting space that speaks to the hearts of potential buyers or renters. As unconventional as these things may seem at first, I promise they are worth doing!

Moving Home Faster Checklist

Preparing the Energy of Your Home

- ☑ Create a welcoming entrance with a clear, inviting doorway
- ☑ Declutter and depersonalize your space to help buyers visualize themselves there
- ☑ Use soft lighting, fresh flowers and earthy tones to enhance warmth and stability
- ☑ Arrange furniture to ensure good energy flow and balance

Ensuring Emotional Readiness and Cord-Cutting

- ☑ Ensure all household members are emotionally ready for the move
- ☑ Have open conversations about the transition, to gain mutual buy-in
- ☑ Perform a cord-cutting visualization exercise to release emotional ties to the home
- ☑ Express gratitude to your home and set an intention for a smooth transition

Setting Clear Intentions for Your Move

- ☑ Write a list of features you want in your future home
- ☑ Start viewing potential homes or researching neighbourhoods

☑ Create a vision board or affirmations to keep your energy high

Decluttering and Staging

☑ Clear out storage areas like the loft, garage, and closets
☑ Organize cupboards and shelves to show spaciousness
☑ Remove excess furniture to create an open and airy feel
☑ Keep surfaces tidy with minimal but intentional décor

Marketing and Attracting Buyers or Renters

☑ Place a "For Sale" or "To Let" sign, if permitted, to signal readiness to the universe
☑ Print out a copy of the property listing and write "SOLD" or "LET" with your ideal price and date
☑ Position a galloping horse at the front door to encourage movement
☑ Use positive language and energy when discussing the sale or rental

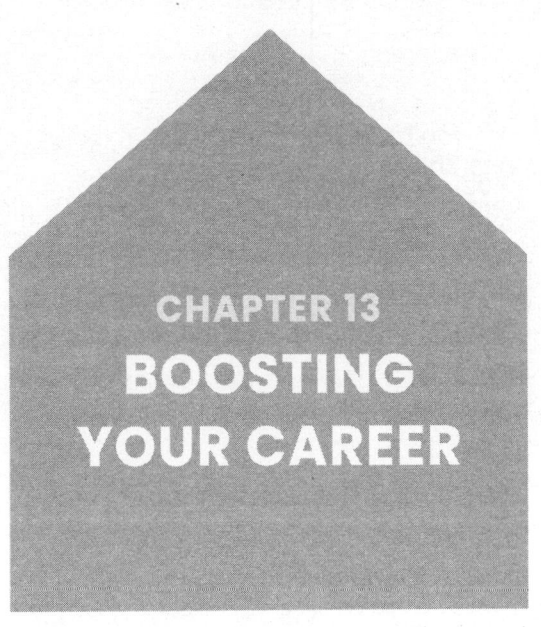

CHAPTER 13
BOOSTING YOUR CAREER

Getting a new job isn't only about updating your CV and applying online; it's also involves creating the right energy to attract new opportunities. Feng Shui helps you do just that by enhancing the space around you in your home, so that it supports your career growth. Simple things like decluttering, concentrating on the North area of your home (which is linked to career success) and adding elements that inspire confidence and ambition can make a big difference. When your environment reflects your goals, you're more likely to see doors open and opportunities come your way.

A few months ago, I received a message on Instagram from Michelle, a woman from the UK who had been searching for a new job. She had come across my podcast, where I talked about how the North area of the home influences careers and business. So, she grabbed a compass, located this area in her home, and realized that, despite moving in 18 months ago, a pile of unpacked moving boxes was still sitting there.

Determined to shift the energy, she cleared the clutter and replaced an old, worn-out stool with a fresh, new one. The very next day, her boyfriend came home from work with unexpected news he had been offered a salary increase and a bonus! Michelle couldn't stop laughing as she told me that while her boyfriend brushed it off as a coincidence, she knew without a doubt that Feng Shui had worked its magic!

So, here are the things that you need to know about how Feng Shui can help you find a new job.

If you are looking to change jobs, have a new career or start a business, you need to look at the North area of your home. And in so much detail that taking an inventory isn't over the top. Sometimes you have things that are just there because they've been there forever and you no longer see them anymore, or perhaps you have forgotten that you even own them. List everything, including any artwork and pictures, and make a note of what these mean to you and how they make you feel when you look at them.

If you don't really give two hoots about the picture on the wall, do you give two hoots about your job? All these items need to match what your aspirations are. What are you wanting to create in your career? Is it to travel? If so, have some artwork that represents travel to you. Is it security? If so, have a picture of something that represents security to you.

I have another version of the "Sustainable Seven" (see page 29) for jobs and careers, and I'd like you to think about three things: mindset, intention and action (MIA).

M is for Mindset

First, let's start with your mindset in your current job, if you have one. On a scale of 1–10, where 1 is very negative and 10 is extremely positive, how do you feel about it?

If you really hate your job then you're likely to be a 1 or a 2. I'm sorry to be the bearer of bad energetic news, but the chances of you getting a new job that you love are very, very slim. Now, don't get me wrong. I've had jobs that I hated and I'm sure most people have had jobs they wished they didn't have.

But if you hate your current job so much that you go in every morning feeling very unmotivated, your thought process is so negative that you're almost frowning and you don't give a hoot what you wear because you don't really care about what you're doing, then I'm afraid all that bad energy is not going to help you get the job of your dreams.

This is your permission to change the narrative about how you feel about your job. I want you to increase that 1 to a 7, even if it's by pretending. Just fake loving your job. Tell yourself you like the people you work with, even if you really don't – Taoism teaches us to go with the ebbs and flows of life and this is doing exactly that. Because as soon as you accept other people's behaviour, whether it's right or wrong, your life will become so much easier.

It's all about changing your energy – and wearing bright clothes is amazing for helping you to lift your mood. Rarely is a work uniform black because designers know the impact this could have on everyone's mood.

So, change what you wear, make an effort, say good morning to everybody and be that ray of sunshine in the office or wherever you work, because doing that is going to lift your own energy level immediately. Keep thinking, "How can I be a Sustainable 7 today at work?", because that is how you're going to attract a new job or a career change.

This is how manifestation works. If you hate your job, you

are not going to be in the necessary mindset or give off the right energy to attract good things back into your life.

I is for Intentions

Moving on to the second component of MIA, what are your intentions?

Rather than just thinking, *"I hate my job"*, what exactly is it that you want to do? You may not know exactly – I didn't either. But you will know how you want to feel. I didn't know what business I actually wanted, but I knew the sorts of things that I wanted to do. For example, I wanted to work completely remotely, to help people, to be financially independent, to love what I do and to be paid on time.

When you think about all these amazing things, it will lift your energy to that Sustainable 7 or maybe even a 9. The higher your energy levels are when you set your intentions using Feng Shui, the more likely you are to attract these things back into your life. (If you would like a recap on how to set your intentions, see Chapter 2.)

Now you need to match your personal energy level with the energy level you feel when you are in the North area of your home.

Crystals can be a really powerful tool in the North area of your home, and if you really dislike your job, then selenite and tourmaline are great at soaking up negative energy. Display them proudly, on your desk, even if colleagues ask, "What on earth are those?" You don't have to justify yourself, but you can always say they are decorative items or you received them as a gift from someone.

A is for Action

The third factor is action, and you need to consider two particular things. First, what you're doing in the North area of your home to attract a new job or a change of career, and second what you are actively doing to find it.

To work, all the expects have to be at 7 out of 10 (or higher!). When you go into the North area of your home, how does it make you feel? Have you dusted recently? I know this is really boring, but I'm afraid a lot of Feng Shui is about clearing space to allow the energy to flow freely, so does this area need decluttering?

When was the last time you cleaned the windows on the inside and outside of the North area of your home? This is where the good energy is coming in, and if you haven't cleaned the windows for ages or you haven't opened them recently, then it's making it really hard for that good energy to come in. Open the door to the North area of your home as well because this allows good energy to flow around the area.

When I'm launching something new in my business, I always do a big declutter, vacuum and mop all the floors, dust everywhere, clean the kitchen thoroughly – especially the stove – all with the intention of welcoming something new into my life. This is particularly important if the North area of your home is where your family comes together, because this could be adding a "hectic" energy to your job or career. If work is quite stressful, adding a salt lamp to this area is an amazing thing to do because it will absorb some of this energy, and don't forget to place tourmaline and selenite crystals there.

Next, I'd like you to think about how you would feel if you got the job of your dreams. Even if you don't know exactly what that is, you will know the feeling and excitement having the job of your dreams would bring. What could you put in the North area of your home that – every time you see it – triggers these feelings? You could place a career vision board here, featuring pictures of things you could do if you got a new job. Adding some fresh flowers would help to bring a growth energy to attract new opportunities. For example, after every TV appearance, I always bring something back like prompt cards or the script and place them in the North area of our home because I'd like to have more of that in my life!

While you want pictures and paintings that lift your energy, I would carefully consider which colours to have in this area. I would try to steer away from lots of images of water. Now, I love pictures of water. I find them really calming, but there is a theory that too much blue or lots of water images can bring too much flow into your life, and good opportunities and money may not stay.

You need to add a little bit of the Fire element, such as small red, yellow or orange décor items in your career area, to bring the energy up, and you also want that energy to come in, especially if you're not feeling very motivated. But I would avoid too many of these because they can bring a feeling of stress and anxiety that you don't require at work.

If there isn't much you can do about the colours, I would add a lovely plant to bring some grounding energy to the area.

Finally, don't forget to add the picture of the Rising Phoenix with your intentions written on the back that we discussed in chapter 1 (see page 22). I like having it near me when I work because seeing it gives me motivation and a little bit of confidence when imposter syndrome creeps in and I start to question myself. When you are looking for or applying for jobs, have that Rising Phoenix around you to boost your confidence – maybe even put it in your bag for the interview!

The wonderful thing about Feng Shui is that you never know what is around the corner. I have no idea where my career is going to take me and what it is going to look like in the future, but I just keep saying out loud "Show me how to share the magic of Feng Shui with as many people around the world as possible". Saying that out loud instantly lifts my energy levels.

Remember, the key is MIA – mindset, intention and action. With all of those things, keep asking yourself if you are hitting a 7 out of 10. Don't get me wrong, I'm sure there will be days when hitting a 2 feels like a really good day. The closer you can get to that 7, the happier you will be, the smoother your work days will be and the more likely it is you're going to attract that amazing job I know is out there for you.

Boosting Your Career Checklist

Assessing Your Space and Decluttering

- ☑ Identify the North area of your home (linked to career success)
- ☑ Take an inventory of everything in this area, including artwork and décor
- ☑ Remove clutter, especially old, broken or unused items
- ☑ Ensure all items reflect your career aspirations (e.g., travel-related images if you want a job with travel)

Shifting Your Mindset

- ☑ Rate your current job satisfaction from 1–10
- ☑ If job satisfaction is low, actively shift your mindset to a Sustainable 7 or above (even if it means pretending)
- ☑ Dress in bright, uplifting colours to boost your mood
- ☑ Engage positively at work – say good morning, bring good energy

Setting Clear Intentions

- ☑ Define what you want in your next job (freedom, security, excitement and so on.)
- ☑ Write down your career intentions and place them in the North area of your home
- ☑ Make a vision board of images that inspire your career goals

Energizing the North Area

- ☑ Clean windows, dust surfaces and clear the space regularly
- ☑ Add elements that attract positive energy, such as:
  - ☑ **Crystals:** Selenite and Tourmaline for clearing negativity
  - ☑ **Salt lamp:** To absorb stressful energy
  - ☑ **Fresh flowers:** To invite growth energy

Taking Inspired Action

- ☑ Actively apply for jobs while maintaining high-energy levels

☑ Place a Rising Phoenix image with your intentions written on the back in the North area

☑ Carry the Rising Phoenix image or a crystal for confidence in job interviews

CHAPTER 14
HAPPY HOLIDAYS

Feng Shui is a powerful way to create harmony, joy and positive energy during celebrations and holidays. Whether it's Halloween, Hanukah, Christmas or any special occasion, the way you decorate and where you place items can either enhance the festive spirit or create a feeling of disorder in the home – something we obviously want to avoid! Decorating mindfully can help you create a home that still feels calm and happy rather than tense and chaotic for both you and your guests.

Finding Balance During the Holiday Season

Before diving into celebrations and Christmas in particular, I want to make something clear – I genuinely love Christmas time! I even did a segment on "The Morning Show" in Australia about Feng Shui and Christmas, and I was very nervous that I might come across as a Christmas grinch! But surprisingly, many people reached out afterwards, grateful for the practical and easy-to-implement tips I shared.

One woman messaged me after the holidays and said, "We had the best Christmas ever, with less red and more natural plants, and everyone commented on how calm and lovely it was." This is exactly what Feng Shui is about – bringing balance into your home so that celebrations feel joyful rather than overwhelming.

While holiday gatherings are filled with love, laughter and tradition, they can also bring stress. From hosting guests to managing family dynamics and dealing with the sheer amount of "stuff" that enters the home (extra decorations, gifts, wrapping paper and toys), it can be a lot. Feng Shui teaches us that these shifts in our environment affect the energy flow in our homes, which in turn impacts how we feel.

During this time of year, it's easy for our homes to become cluttered, which can lead to a sense of being overwhelmed. One of the best things you can do before decorating is a deep declutter, making space for the new energy the holiday season will bring. Let go of any broken decorations, unused ornaments or holiday items that no longer bring you joy. This simple act alone can help improve the energy of your home before the festivities even begin.

Preparing Your Home for Holiday Décor

Before adding any holiday decorations, take a moment to assess your space. How does your home feel right now? What colours are dominant? What's the current energy like? Making small adjustments before introducing new elements can help ensure that your holiday décor enhances, rather than disrupts, the energy of your home.

One of the biggest areas to focus on is colour. In Feng Shui, fiery colours like red, hot pink, burned orange, purple and burgundy fall under the Fire element. These colours bring warmth and excitement, but too much of them can lead to heightened emotions, stress and even arguments.

If your holidays are typically full of joy and relaxation, then you don't need to worry about using fiery tones. However, if past holidays have been stressful or tense, it may be worth reconsidering your colour palette.

I'll be honest, when I first started learning about Feng Shui, all of our red decorations mysteriously "went missing". Instead, I opted for gold, white and soft metallics, which align with the Metal element known for absorbing negative energy. If you're looking for a more peaceful holiday experience, try incorporating these shades into your décor.

If you love traditional red décor for Christmas, but feel that tensions are rising, start removing some red elements one by one until you notice a shift in the energy. This doesn't mean you have to abandon the "Christmas red" festive colours altogether, just find a balance that works for your home.

Wrapping Paper and Gift Presentation

The colours and textures of your wrapping paper also contribute to the overall energy in your home. Consider using metallics, soft blues, whites and golds, which feel festive without being overwhelming. Wrapping gifts in calming colours sets a serene and welcoming tone for Christmas morning or any gift-giving celebration.

Another great Feng Shui practice is to wrap gifts with intention. When wrapping, take a moment to think about the person receiving the gift and infuse it with positive energy. If possible, opt for reusable gift wrap or eco-friendly materials to keep the energy of giving in harmony with nature.

The Power of Candles and Scents

Candles add warmth and ambiance to holiday décor but be mindful of placement. In Feng Shui, the Centre of your home represents health and balance. Placing candles in this area can symbolically "burn off" the home's good health energy, which we definitely don't want – especially during the flu season!

Instead, place candles in other areas of your home and opt for natural, toxin-free varieties to keep the energy pure. To create a festive scent for Christmas without artificial chemicals, try simmering a pot of water, adding cloves, cinnamon, orange slices and star anise. It fills your home with a beautiful aroma while adding to the cosy atmosphere.

Artificial vs Natural Decorations

If you've been following me for a while on social media, you know I usually avoid artificial plants because they lack life and energy. However, Christmas presents a bit of a challenge as many of us have artificial trees, wreaths and garlands. When we moved to Australia, I was devastated to learn that keeping a real Christmas tree alive in the summer heat was nearly impossible. So, I had to make peace with an artificial one. My general rule now is: if it's just for the season, it's OK.

To balance artificial decorations, try incorporating real elements like fresh greenery, flowers or white poinsettias. Your front door is an important area in Feng Shui as it's where positive energy enters your home. If you hang a wreath on your door, consider one made of fresh foliage rather than an artificial one that has spiky holly and red berries, which can create sharp and stagnant energy.

As an alternative, you could try making a wreath made

of battery-powered lights, because it's warm, welcoming and doesn't carry the "sharp" or stagnant energy of artificial décor.

Managing Family Gatherings with Feng Shui

Holiday gatherings can be wonderful but also stressful times, especially when hosting guests with different personalities and energy levels. One way to create a harmonious atmosphere is through the strategic use of Feng Shui elements.

Crystals: Crystals are fantastic for absorbing negative energy. A selenite sphere on your dining table not only looks like a festive snowball but also helps maintain a calm and peaceful atmosphere. If you're worried about difficult guests, black tourmaline is an excellent grounding crystal – though it does look a little like a lump of coal! If needed, you can discreetly pop some under chairs for your more challenging guests!

Table Décor: Placing a real plant, candle or fresh foliage in the centre of the dining table helps ground the energy. Playing calming background music can also subtly shift the energy in the room, promoting more relaxed and enjoyable conversations.

Dressing for the Holidays: Choosing Colours Mindfully

What we wear impacts our personal energy, and as holiday outfits often feature red, it's worth considering how this fiery colour affects you. If red isn't a colour you usually wear, don't feel pressured to wear it just because it's Christmas. Instead, opt for grounding tones like green or white.

Similarly, if your holiday table is covered in red décor, try swapping out table runners, napkins or candle holders for gold, silver or green. Small adjustments like this can make a big difference to the overall energy of your celebrations.

Planning Ahead for a Stress-Free Holiday Season

One of the simplest ways to reduce stress during the holidays is to plan ahead. Make a shopping list in advance to avoid a last-minute panic and set realistic expectations for yourself. Most importantly, create an environment that feels good to you and your family. The holidays are about joy, connection and creating memories, and sometimes simple Feng Shui adjustments can make all the difference for a calm, happy and harmonious festive season.

Happy Holiday Checklist

Decluttering First and Choosing Colours Wisely

- ☑ Clear out old, broken or unused decorations before bringing in new festive items
- ☑ Balance fiery red tones with calming golds, whites and metallics for a harmonious space

Choosing Décor and Using Natural Elements

- ☑ Assess your home's energy before decorating and ensure new elements enhance the flow

☑ Incorporate real greenery, fresh flowers or natural wreaths to balance artificial decorations

Wrapping Gifts Mindfully and Placing Candles Strategically

☑ Use soft blues, whites, and metallics for a serene energy, and wrap gifts with intention

☑ To protect balanced energy, avoid placing candles in the Centre of the home

Creating a Harmonious Table Setting and Managing Family Energy

☑ Add fresh plants, candles or calming crystals like selenite to ground energy

☑ Use black tourmaline to absorb negativity, and play soothing background music

Dressing for Balance and Planning Ahead

☑ Wear grounding colours like green or white instead of overstimulating red if you feel stressed

☑ Set realistic expectations, make lists and create a holiday environment that feels joyful and calm

CHAPTER 15
DOS AND DON'TS AROUND THE HOME

I'm going to walk you through the house and highlight the key areas I focus on first when working with a client. Also, if you are short on time, this is the perfect place to start.

The Entrance to Your Home

Starting with the outside of your home, the front entrance needs to be as clear as possible, whether that's a pathway or a communal entrance, because that is where the good energy comes into the home. If the energy has to work really hard to navigate around lots of trash, mess, dead weeds and leaves, it's going to make it difficult for it to enter your home.

As you enter, make sure that your front door opens easily. If it doesn't, it's making it difficult to get into your home and for the good energy to come in. Make sure that the door doesn't stick and the lock opens easily, and that you have a clean, easy entrance into your home so that good energy can easily flow in. While you are there, check that the door handle is sturdy and not wobbly as a loose handle represents a feeling of instability and a lack of control. If you have an entrance mat, ensure it's clean and inviting. A mat with a welcoming message, such as "Welcome" is perfect. However, if your mat is outside, check it isn't dirty or worn out. A mat that collects mud, dust and dirt can carry negative energy into your home, especially when it's windy or you step on it and bring it in with you.

Next, inspect your windows – they need to be clean both on the inside and outside, and if your front door has a window, that too should be clean. This also applies to any rooms around your house where you have doors with windows in them. Otherwise, the dirt can prevent good energy from entering and circulating around your home.

Outside Your Home

Unfortunately, most of the time you can't control what happens outside your home. If you want to stop specific negative energy from entering, you can add a wind chime to the entrance. This can be used if, for example, you live on a busy road, or you want to stop energy from your neighbours entering your home.

If you don't like wind chimes or it's not possible to have one, try placing a tourmaline and selenite crystal in or by your entrance. These act like big sponges and absorb all negative energy. They also help to cleanse the area.

Another big thing to look out for is stagnant water outside your home. The theory is that running water brings in wealth, abundance and prosperity and the opposite is true for stagnant water – it can negatively impact your wealth.

One lady I worked with had eight water butts full of stagnant water that she got rid of from the bottom of her garden. Not long after this, her husband was offered a new job! Another person cleared stagnant energy from her garden by emptying plant pots, buckets and furniture of stagnant water that had accumulated. She emptied it all and her son, who lives at home, was offered a job that day. It is unbelievably powerful!

It's also important to think about your garage if you have one, because whatever is in there holds on to energy. Quite often (and I am guilty of this), we put things in there that we no longer use or no longer desire to have in our home. Ask yourself this, if it doesn't deserve a place in your home, what is it doing in your garage? If you are going to use it again then that's fine but, if not, it's time to think about giving it a new home because its stagnant energy will be seeping into your home, especially if you have an integrated garage.

Outdoor and Indoor Bins

Many of us have to have bins outside the entrance to our home. If this is the case for you and you have to walk past your bins to go into your home, see if you can put them in some sort of covered storage. Not only are they unsightly, but the energy of whatever is in the bin could be making its way into your home – and we absolutely don't want that. If you could move them around to the side of your home, it would make a huge difference. Out of sight, out of mind.

This brings me on to bins inside your home. Obviously, we empty our kitchen bins quite often, because we're around them all the time. Maybe they smell, they're not attractive, the recycling gets full and you're always taking them out – which is great because you don't want their energy circulating around your home. But this also applies to your bathroom bins – and I'm really bad at this. I will leave things in bathroom bins because I genuinely forget to empty them. I'm not saying you need to empty them daily, but it's definitely something to have in your routine every couple of days, just to take that energy out of your home.

Hallways

Your hallway is the next key area to consider, as it acts as a corridor for energy to flow through your home. It's so easy for hallways to become cluttered with coats, shoes and bags. To avoid this, try to store these items elsewhere. For example, I moved bulky winter coats to hooks on the back of a door in another room.

As for shoes, we store most of ours in our wardrobes and only keep out the pairs we use daily. I'm not a fan of open shoe racks because the energy from the shoes can still enter the home. Instead, opt for an enclosed storage solution, such as a laundry bin with a lid. This is a way to store shoes in the hallway if you don't have another place for them. Just be sure to clean them before putting them away – I know that sounds overly meticulous, but I don't think of it as only cleaning, I see it as managing energy. If dirt symbolizes stagnant or messy energy, then I don't want it in my home!

Mirrors are often placed in hallways, and there are many different beliefs about them in Feng Shui – some positive, some not. They can be beneficial as they reflect space and create a more open and airier feel. However, it's best to avoid positioning them directly opposite windows, as this can reflect good energy straight back out. That said, sometimes it's simply unavoidable. For example, when we lived in the UK, the only place we could position a mirror in our bedroom was directly opposite a window. Therefore, while this chapter is about Feng Shui dos and don'ts, the real takeaway is: do what you can and if something can't be changed, don't stress about it!

Staircases

Stairs that are directly opposite your front door are considered less than ideal in Feng Shui and here's why. The front door is known as the "mouth of Chi," the entry point for all the good energy flowing into your home. When stairs are positioned directly opposite, that energy tends to rush up or down the staircase, and it misses out the rest of the house. This can make it a bit tricky to keep positive energy in the home, as well as attract wealth and opportunities. Instead of circulating through the home, the energy leaves as quickly as it enters. If the stairs lead to an upper floor, the energy might seem overly concentrated up there, leaving the ground floor feeling neglected. If the stairs lead to a basement, it can feel as if the energy is sinking, which may make you feel like life is stagnant or even moving backward.

But please don't worry. I always believe there is a way around everything. You can place a rug or a small piece of furniture, a plant or even a crystal there, if you don't have much room to deflect the energy. Another trick is to add artwork or mirrors to the stair wall. Artwork slows the upward flow of energy, while mirrors (positioned carefully though, so they're not directly reflecting the door) can help redirect energy into the rest of the home.

Plants – What to Have and What to Avoid

A topic that always causes controversy is artificial plants. I did a segment on "This Morning" about them, which was a lot of fun as Dermot O'Leary (one of the presenters) ended up collecting all the fake plants and throwing them off the set on live TV! Feng Shui is all about life and energy, so anything that is fake is the complete opposite to this, and artificial plants can bring a feeling of stagnation into the home.

Now don't get me wrong, there are some beautiful artificial flowers that you would never know aren't real, but if you are wanting to create that feeling of life and energy in your home, then I would suggest adding real plants.

In Feng Shui, cacti are a bit tricky. While they can be beautiful and low maintenance, their sharp spikes can bring what's known as "sha chi" or negative energy. The spiky energy they emit isn't exactly the kind you want flowing through your home. The sharpness of cacti is thought to symbolize cutting or defensive energy, which can stir up tension or conflict. If you're looking to create a calm and harmonious environment, placing a cactus in spaces like the bedroom, living room or anywhere relationships and connection are key, might not be the best idea. You want these spaces to feel cosy and inviting, not prickly! Cacti are also considered bad news when it comes to prosperity and luck. In Feng Shui, wealth and abundance thrive on smooth, flowing energy, so I'd say it's wise not to have them in or around your home.

So what plants *should* you have? It's fair to say that I am pretty bad at keeping plants alive and my horticultural knowledge is less than average. The simple rule to follow is to make sure that the plants you choose grow upward, as these represent strength, and not down, as these symbolize energy pulling us down. Ideal choices would be any that have lovely soft green leaves, such as money plants.

This goes for your garden as well, because this energy will be entering your home through the doors and windows. If your home has wisteria or ivy growing around it, this can bring an overwhelming feeling, even suffocation, into the home – as if you can't breathe. I admit it can look very pretty, but in Feng Shui it's seen as strangling the home and stopping the building from breathing. Whenever I see a house covered in ivy and wisteria, I get the feeling it's like wearing a itchy polo neck that makes you really hot and bothered, and you just want to pull it off!

I had a message, from a lady, Camille, to say she had got rid of all of their ivy, plants and trees growing up around the house. She said it felt as if they could breathe again and they no longer felt overwhelmed and suffocated by life.

I hope this helps you to make some quick changes that bring fresh, positive vibes into your space. Feng Shui doesn't have to be complicated – small tweaks like decluttering, adding plants and being mindful of how energy moves through your home can make a big difference.

Dos and Don'ts Checklist

Dos

☑ Keep your entrance clear and welcoming – this is where all the good energy comes in, so no clutter, dead plants or mess

☑ Check your front door – make sure it opens easily, the handle is sturdy and the mat is clean and inviting

☑ Use wind chimes or crystals at the entrance – great for blocking unwanted energy from busy roads or neighbours

☑ Keep windows and mirrors clean – let the light and energy flow freely

☑ **Clear stagnant water** – whether it's a forgotten bucket in the garden or a dripping tap, water should move, not sit!

☑ **Empty bins regularly** – especially bathroom bins (I know, I forget too!)

☑ **Store shoes in a closed space** – open shoe racks near the entrance? Not ideal for energy flow

☑ **Fix leaks** – money and opportunities could be slipping away with that dripping tap

☑ **Declutter your garage** – if it's not worthy of your home, why keep it in your garage?

☑ **Work with what you've got** – if you can't move something, don't stress. Feng Shui is about balance, not perfection.

Don'ts

☑ **Don't block your front door** – if energy struggles to get in, so will opportunities

☑ **Avoid mirrors directly opposite windows** – we don't want all that good energy bouncing straight back out!

☑ **No dried or artificial plants** – real plants bring good energy. Fake plants – not so much

☑ **Avoid keeping bins at the entrance** – if you have to, put them in a covered storage unit

☑ **Don't let clutter pile up in hallways** – this is the energy's pathway, so keep it flowing

☑ **No broken or wobbly door handles** – it represents instability in life

☑ **Avoid placing mirrors directly opposite the front door** – you don't want energy rushing straight back out

☑ **Don't panic if you can't follow every rule** – do what works for your home and lifestyle!

CHAPTER 16
CRYSTALS FOR FENG SHUI

Crystals have been used for centuries to enhance energy, promote healing and bring balance to our spaces. When combined with the principles of Feng Shui, crystals become even more powerful tools for creating harmony and well-being in the home. Each of the Nine Areas of the home corresponds to different aspects of life (see chapter 2) and by placing specific crystals in these areas, you can amplify their positive effects. Below, we explore the nine areas of the home and the best crystals for optimal energy flow.

North – Career, Business and Life's Journey

Crystals: Black Obsidian and Lapis Lazuli
Black obsidian is a powerful grounding stone that absorbs negative energy and provides clarity and protection in your professional journey. It helps remove obstacles and clears stagnant energy that may be blocking progress.

Lapis lazuli is a lovely deep-blue stone that enhances wisdom and encourages self-expression. It helps in decision-making and improves communication, making it an excellent stone for those looking to advance in their careers.

Northeast – Knowledge, Wisdom, Personal Growth, Learning, Intuition

Crystals: Amethyst and Fluorite
Amethyst is known for its calming and intuitive properties, helping to deepen concentration and enhance clarity of thought. It fosters inner peace and spiritual development.

Fluorite, with its vibrant mix of colours, is excellent for mental clarity and focus. It helps with organization and decision-making, making it ideal for study and workspaces or areas where learning takes place.

East – Family and Community

Crystals: Green Aventurine and Moss Agate
Green aventurine is known as the "Stone of Opportunity", bringing vitality and optimism. It supports overall well-being in the home, while also fostering harmony within the family.

Moss agate has a strong connection to nature and is believed to have healing properties that reduce stress and promote emotional balance. It's especially beneficial for strengthening family bonds and improving communication.

Southeast – Wealth, Prosperity, Abundance, Success and Financial Growth

Crystals: Citrine and Pyrite
Citrine, known as the "Merchant's Stone", attracts financial success and personal power. It carries the energy of the sun, bringing joy, confidence and abundance.

Pyrite, also called "Fool's Gold", symbolizes luck and prosperity. It encourages wealth-building and protection against financial setbacks, making it a great crystal for business owners or those looking to improve financial stability.

South – Fame, Reputation, Recognition and Self-Worth

Crystals: Tiger's Eye and Carnelian
Tiger's eye is a stone of courage and motivation, helping you overcome fear and self-doubt. It enhances willpower and attracts success, making it ideal for those looking to gain visibility in their careers.

Carnelian, a fiery orange crystal, ignites passion, creativity and confidence. It is particularly useful for artists, performers and anyone who wants to make a lasting impression in their field.

Southwest – Love and Relationships

Crystals: Rose Quartz and Rhodonite
(**Note:** Make sure you always use two of these crystals to represent the two people in a relationship.)

Rose quartz, the ultimate stone of love, fosters deep emotional healing and attracting loving relationships. It strengthens existing bonds and promotes self-love.

Rhodonite is another heart-centred stone that helps heal emotional wounds and promotes forgiveness. Rhodonite encourages balance in relationships and helps to resolve conflicts with compassion.

West – Children, Fertility and New Beginnings

Crystals: Orange Calcite and Selenite
Orange calcite is a powerful energizing stone that enhances

creativity and removes self-doubt. It's perfect for artistic spaces or for those looking to reignite their passion for creative projects.

Selenite, with its elegant glow, brings clarity and peace. It promotes a sense of purity and lightness, making it ideal for children's rooms or areas where new ideas and inspiration flow.

Northwest – Helpful People and Travel

Crystals: Hematite and Labradorite
Hematite is a grounding and protective stone that strengthens connections with influential people and stabilizes energy in social interactions.

Labradorite, known for its mesmerizing flashes of colour, is a stone of transformation and intuition. It enhances spiritual awareness and supports those seeking guidance or embarking on new adventures.

Centre – Physical and Mental Health and Overall Well-Being

Crystals: Clear Quartz and Smoky Quartz
Clear quartz is known as the "Master Healer", as it amplifies the energy of all other crystals. It brings clarity, purification and high vibrations, making it an essential crystal for maintaining well-being.

Smoky quartz is excellent for grounding and dispelling negativity. It helps absorb stress and anxiety, promoting a sense of stability and calm in the heart of your home.

Bringing It All Together

By placing these crystals in their respective areas, you create a home filled with positive, balanced energy. But be sure to cleanse your crystals regularly to maintain their effectiveness– for example, using sage, moonlight or sunlight – because crystals can absorb and store energy from their environment, including negative or stagnant energy. Over time, this accumulation can reduce the crystal's effectiveness or block its healing properties. Trust your intuition when placing them and remember that Feng Shui is all about flow and your home reflecting the energy you wish to invite into your life.

CHAPTER 17

TIPS FOR QUICK AND EASY FIXES

This section is a summary and reference guide of quick and easy Feng Shui fixes to help different areas of your life, including your finances, your health and your sleep.

Money Tips

Tie Red Ribbon around Pipes

In Feng Shui, tying red ribbon around pipes is like putting a little protective seal on your energy flow, especially when it comes to money. It's all about symbolically stopping your wealth from draining away.

Clean the Stove

The kitchen is closely linked to wealth and prosperity, and it is believed that the stove is where some of the wealth energy comes from. Keeping the stove clean will allow wealth energy to enter your home. But here is a little tip – make sure that when you clean the stove you are thinking about bringing more money into your home. Believe it or not, after posting a reel on this, I've had nearly 100 people message me to say that they received unexpected money from doing this – from lottery wins to tax rebates!

Declutter Your Kitchen

The kitchen represents wealth and prosperity, this area needs to be as clean and clear as possible to allow the energy to circulate. Also remove any broken or chipped dishes because this could impact the healthy flow of prosperity in the home.

Fix any Leaks and Dripping Taps

Leaking water means leaking wealth in Feng Shui. Therefore, check all pipes, showers, taps and even gutters to make sure that money isn't draining away.

Keep the Toilet Seat Lid Down

This tends to be the one Feng Shui tip that people have heard of before because it relates to money going down the drain. Keep the toilet lid closed to stop money draining away.

Invite Good Energy In

The good energy that brings wealth (as well as health) into your home enters via your front door, so make sure that this area is inviting. It should be clear, clean and well-lit to invite this energy in.

Use Mirrors Wisely

Avoid having mirrors directly opposite the front door as this will bounce the good energy and potentially your finances right back out of your home. Instead have a picture that brings you joy and happiness

Keep Your Wallet in Good Order

Keep your wallet clear of clutter and get rid of old receipts. Also make sure it's not worn out and tatty. Your wallet is a home for your money, and it should feel inviting and abundant!

Add Plants to the Wealth Corner

Place healthy, green plants (like a jade plant or money tree) in the Southeast corner of your home because this area is linked to wealth. Avoid thorny plants like cacti here – they might "prick" your finances. And most definitely avoid artificial or dried flowers in this area, because these could stagnate your finances.

Make a Modern Wealth Bowl

Place a glass candle holder on top of a mirrored candle plate and add money, crystals such as citrine or pyrite and anything else you would like to welcome into your life. The mirror helps to "double" this energy, so place it in the Southeast area of your home.

Sleep Tips

Declutter

A tidy space allows the energy to flow freely but calmly around your room. Try not to leave piles of clothes on the chair or laundry that needs to be put away, because this will prevent energy from circulating in your bedroom.

Position Your Bed Carefully

The ideal position for a bed is to have it in the "command position" against a solid wall where you can see the door. This will give you a feeling of solidarity while helping you to relax knowing that you can see whatever is coming your way. However, don't sleep directly opposite the door because the energy will be coming at you, which can disrupt your sleep.

I fully understand that it's not always possible to move the bed, so if you do have to sleep directly opposite the door, place a rug on the floor in between the bed and the door or add a fluffy throw to your bed to help slow down the energy a little. Also, having a small gap in between the bed and the wall will help the energy to flow slowly and freely around you all night, without it getting stuck. Therefore, leaving just a small gap behind the headboard is perfect. Avoid sleeping under a window, if possible, as this can give a fragile energy to those who sleep underneath it. If you have no option other than to place your bed under a window, I recommend having a solid headboard to give you support.

Open all Windows and Drapes or Blinds in the Day

Energy enters the home through the doors and windows, so having rooms that remain dark all day with the drapes closed will eventually feel "stale". This is simply because no new energy can enter, and the old energy remains and becomes stagnant. I recommend that every day you open the drapes or blinds and windows (even if it's just for 30 seconds if you live in a cold climate) and it will make all the difference.

Close the Door at Night

If you really struggle to sleep, try closing your door when you sleep. The idea is that this prevents energy from entering the room and creates a stillness while you sleep.

Choose Calming Colours for Bed Linen

What colour is your bed linen? All colours have an energy; some are calm and some are more energetic. When it comes to your bed, go for calmer tones that belong to the Earth family, such as creams and beiges, or those that belong to the Wood family, such as greens. If you like patterns, I recommend a flowing or wavy pattern, avoiding anything with points or angular shapes.

Put Away Work (or School) Clothes

Whether you love or loathe your job, your work clothes will hold the energy from the day and placing these in your room while you sleep will have an impact on how you feel in your bedroom. The same applies to children and their school clothes. Make sure that when you finish your workday (and the children their school day), everyone puts their clothes away. You can designate a small separate section in the wardrobe where "worn but not dirty" clothes can go if you don't want them next to clean clothes.

Tidy Away Work and Workout Equipment

Working in the bedroom can give off an energy of exhaustion, even if you love your job. If you do work in your bedroom, make sure that at the end of every day you put away any work items because this will help you to switch off from your job. There are some amazing put-up desks available online that are easy to pop up in the morning and put away at the end of the day.

Check Artwork

Artwork in the bedroom should be as calming as possible, sticking to soothing tones and soft lines. I would also opt for pictures that represent pairs of things or people, to really enhance the feeling of partnership and friendship in the home. For example, for the adult bedroom, either a couple walking and holding hands or pairs of animals who have mates for life, such as swans or ducks. Pictures of peonies are also lovely as they represent love and romance. In children's rooms, opt for images of more than one person, animal or item to promote friendship.

Clear under the Beds

The energy of anything stored under the bed will be able to make its way up through the mattress and could impact sleep. If you must store items there, only keep soft items like bedding, towels, jumpers and so on – not shoes or bags.

Declutter Bedside Tables and Cabinets

Make sure that bedside tables aren't overflowing with items because this will cause the energy to get stuck. Put books away at night – especially if they are written about people having lots of affairs! Personally, I can't sleep with crystals near my bed because they can be so powerful that they disrupt my sleep. It's worth putting them in a corner away from your bed if you struggle to sleep.

Beware the Effects of Electronics

Try not to store these by the bed because they will obviously give off an electrical energy while you sleep. If this isn't possible, you could try sleeping on a grounding sheet – these go under your fitted sheet and ground any electrical energy that surrounds you. There is also lots of research to suggest that they really do help with sleep, inflammation headaches and even menopause symptoms.

Limit Plants

Plants can be a really lovely addition to the bedroom. However, because they are alive and growing, they obviously give off energy. In other areas of the house, this is exactly what you want, but in the bedroom we are trying to slow everything down. So, if you love plants in the bedroom, limit yourself to one and make sure that it has soft leaves (no spikes) and grows upward.

Unplug TVs

Sorry to be the bearer of bad news, but TVs can impact our sleep for two reasons. One is that they are electrical and give off energy into the bedroom and the other is that because of their reflective nature they can speed up the energy in the room. That said, please don't worry if you do have a TV in your room – we inherited the world's biggest TV in our bedroom when we bought our house, which obviously isn't ideal, so I just keep it unplugged.

Lessen the Energy of Mirrors

Just like the TV, the mirrors speed up the energy in the bedroom. Now, I know that many homes have mirrored wardrobes (including my daughter's room). Firstly, if you sleep fine, then don't worry about it. If you do struggle, we just need to try to slow down the energy a little. This can be done by adding rugs or throws to the end of the bed. You can obviously try and cover the mirror if you wish, but I do think it's quite extreme, not to mention a chore, to be hanging massive sheets over your wardrobe every night!

Avoid Family Photos

Try not to have family photos in your bedroom if you can because, even the photos have an energy. Also, you don't want people looking over at you in the bedroom! If you really want to have photos up, turn them so that they aren't looking directly at you.

Respect Religious Items

It is not recommended to have any religious items in the bedroom out of respect. This is mainly because you don't want them "seeing" into what constitutes a private space. Anywhere else in the home is absolutely fine.

Health and Well-Being Tips

Centre of the Home

The Centre of the home looks after our overall health, both our physical and mental health, but also self-acceptance and confidence. So, it's a pretty important part of the home to look after. The first thing to do is to ensure that this area is as clutter-free as possible to allow the energy to circulate and not get stuck. It is believed that stagnant energy in this area can add to health issues because no new energy is rejuvenating this area of our life. Keeping medicines in the Centre can be seen as a "self-fulfilling prophecy," in that you are creating an energy of needing those medicines to keep healthy. If you can, store them out of sight and not in the Centre of your home.

Stairs in the Centre

If you have stairs in the Centre of the home, it is believed that this can bring an "up-and-down" energy to your health, almost as if you are constantly battling with health challenges in the home. Don't worry, I'm not going to ask you to move the stairs! But we need to try slow down this energy and we can do that by adding a plant around the bottom of the stairs to help ground the energy. I would also avoid having mirrors in the centre of the staircase, as this may add to the speed of the energy.

Kitchen in the Centre

Due to the amount of fiery energy in the kitchen, if this room is in the Centre of the home, it may bring a feeling of being burned out. This really isn't a nice feeling at all, so if you are experiencing this (and even if your kitchen isn't in the Centre), I would add a plant or two to the kitchen to try to ground some of this energy.

Front Entrance

Lovely fresh energy enters your home through your front entrance, so make sure that it can get into and around your home. Opening the door daily to welcome in the good energy will make a huge difference to your home. Then clearing as much as you can in your entrance will ensure the energy can enter freely. This goes for outside your home; make sure that your pathway is clear and any weeds and dead plants are removed.

Windows

As well as through the front door, good energy comes in through the windows, so it's really important that these are kept clean. I have to admit, cleaning windows is right at the bottom of the jobs I like to do because I can never get rid of all the smears. However, when I do clean them, I notice the big difference this makes to the energy in that room.

Artificial Plants

Feng Shui is about life and new energy, so if you feel that you are getting nowhere with your health and you have artificial plants in the Centre of your home, I recommend giving them away.

Spiky Plants

Spiky plants such as cacti can give off a prickly and spiky energy in the home, which can leave you feeling on edge. These plants aren't recommended, especially if anyone in the home suffers with anxiety. Sticky to lovely leafy, soft and upward-growing plants.

Lighting

Due to the location of the centre of the home, you might find that it lacks natural light. If this is the case in your home, you can layer your lighting. This means having some different options such as up-lights and candles, as well as the main lighting in the area. Mirrors will also help to reflect the light around the space.

Opening Doors, Drapes and Windows

We need to promote new and fresh energy in the Centre of the home so that we are making the most of the health energy in the home, especially if you feel that yours could do with waking up a little. Ensure that all doors are open in the day, to allow the energy to circulate, and open the drapes and windows daily too.

Artwork Symbolizing Health

What does "health" mean to you? Whatever that is, place artwork or pictures in the Centre of the home as a visual affirmation to represent how you want your health to be.

It might be pictures of a time when you didn't have health challenges, or perhaps something you would like to do when your physical or mental health improves.

Looking deeper into the areas of the home, some are linked to more specific areas of our body and also people. In addition to the above tips, you could revisit chapter 2 and go through the points above in each of these areas.

CHAPTER 18
DECLUTTER CHECKLIST

As you know by now, decluttering is a fundamental part of Feng Shui. However, I completely understand that the process can feel overwhelming. That's why I've created this checklist, which breaks down your home into manageable areas. By tackling one section at a time, you'll create a more balanced and harmonious energy flow throughout your space, making a noticeable difference in how your home feels.

1. Preparation and Mindset

☑ **Set Your Intention:** Note down what you wish to welcome into your home – whether it's more peace, success, health or happiness

☑ **Choose a Start Date:** Pick a day when you can work without interruptions. But remember, it doesn't all have to be done in a day – just 15 minutes a day will make a huge difference

☑ **Gather Supplies:** Get together boxes for charity donations, storage containers, cleaning products and a small bin bag for each room to keep things manageable.

2. Entrance Tidy-Up – when you enter your home, it should feel like you are coming into your sanctuary

☑ **Clear Clutter at the Door:** Remove extra shoes, bags and anything blocking the entrance to allow energy to flow in freely

☑ **Create a Warm Welcome:** Place a plant, crystals or artwork that brings you joy and happiness near the door to create an inviting feel

☑ **Organize Shoe and Coat Storage:** Tidy the shoe rack and coat cupboard, donating or discarding any unused items. Have you worn them in the last year? If not, then it's time to give them to a new home

3. Sitting Room Refresh – this area needs to feel as relaxing as possible

☑ **Clear Surfaces:** Declutter books, magazines and ornaments, keeping only items that bring joy or relaxation

☑ **Rearrange Furniture:** Position seating to encourage easy movement and comfortable conversation

☑ **Freshen Décor:** Add in or rotate new cushions, blankets, or plants to give the room a fresh feel

4. Kitchen Clear-Out – the kitchen is linked to prosperity, so this is a really important room in the house

☑ **Take Stock of Cupboard and Fridge:** Remove out-of-date food and consider donating unused and unwanted items

☑ **Organize Cabinets:** Group items for easy access, with daily essentials to hand

☑ **Keep Counters Clear:** Only leave out daily-use items to support a calm, clear mind while cooking

5. Bedroom Sanctuary – the bedroom is for romance, rest and relaxation, not for working or working out

☑ **Tidy around the Bed:** Clear anything stored under the bed (if possible) to allow smooth energy flow

☑ **Refresh Your Wardrobe:** Sort clothes and donate or repurpose what no longer suits your style. Don't beat yourself up by keeping clothes that no longer fit you!

☑ **Keep the Bedside Table Simple:** Limit to essentials – perhaps a lamp, a small plant and a journal – definitely no books about people having multiple affairs!

6. Bathroom Declutter – this is the one I always dread!

☑ **Clear Surfaces:** Tidy up toiletries, removing any out-of-date products or empty bottles. Most beauty products have a one-year shelf life!

☑ **Organize Cupboards:** Group items by type and throw out any clutter

☑ **Add Natural Touches:** A small plant or wooden item brings life and vitality into the space

7. Office or Study Space Tidy-Up

☑ **Clear out Paper:** Sort through files, papers and notebooks. Digitize where possible and recycle what you don't need

☑ **Keep Desk Essentials Only:** Keep only daily essentials on the desk – like your laptop, a notebook and your favourite pen – to stay focused. An amethyst is a lovely crystal to help with concentration, and of course my all-time favourites are selenite and tourmaline to absorb negativity

☑ **Organize Electronics:** Tidy up cables and chargers to create an open, energizing workspace

8. Digital Declutter – this one is very important because we spend so much time on our phones!

☑ **Clear Out Your Inbox:** Delete old emails, unsubscribe from unnecessary lists and organize important folders. How many emails do you have?!

☑ **Re-Organize Your Phone and Computer:** Delete unused apps, old photos and unnecessary files; install updates and organize your desktop for a fresh start

☑ **Audit Social Media:** Unfollow any accounts that don't inspire or align with you. This feels so good!

9. Final Touches

☑ **Cleanse Energy:** Use sage, incense or essential oils in a diffuser to refresh the energy in your home.

☑ **Open the Windows:** Let in fresh air to shift any stagnant energy

☑ **Positive Reminders:** Place affirmation cards, inspiring quotes or small visual affirmations around the home in the nine different areas.

I hope this book helps to bring you the calm and happiness you deserve in your home.

So Much Love,

Kimberley xx

the feng shui flow™

WITH KIMBERLEY GALLAGHER

REFERENCES

Amazon. (2025). *Bestsellers in Healthy Living & Wellness.* Amazon. https://www.amazon.com.au/gp/bestsellers/books/4894554051/ref=zg_b_bs_4894554051_1

Ashburner, J, Ziviani, J, & Rodger, S (2013). Sensory processing and classroom emotional, behavioural, and educational outcomes in children with autism spectrum disorder. *American Journal of Occupational Therapy, 62(5), 564–73*

Boubekri, M, Cheung, I N, Reid, K J, Wang, C H, & Zee, P C (2014). Impact of windows and daylight exposure on overall health and sleep quality of office workers: A case-control pilot study. *Journal of Clinical Sleep Medicine, 10(6), 603-611.*

Capaldi, C A, Passmore, H A, Nisbet, E K, Zelenski, J M, & Dopko, R L (2015). Flourishing in nature: A review of the benefits of connecting with nature and its application as a wellbeing intervention. *International Journal of Wellbeing, 5(4)*

Figueiro, M G, Steverson, B, Heerwagen, J, Kampschroer, K, Hunter, C M, Gonzales, K, & Rea, M S (2017). The impact of light on outcomes in healthcare settings. *Herd.*

Küller, R, Ballal, S, Laike, T, Mikellides, B, & Tonello, G (2009). The impact of light and colour on psychological mood: A cross-cultural study of indoor work environments. *Ergonomics , 49(14): 1496–507*

Saxbe, D E, & Repetti, R L (2010). No place like home: Home tours correlate with daily patterns of mood and cortisol. *Personality and Social Psychology Bulletin , 36(1), 71–81*

Wolverton, B C, Johnson, A, & Bounds, K (1989). *Interior landscape plants for indoor air pollution abatement.* NASA, Stennis Space Center

ACKNOWLEDGEMENTS

Writing this book has been an incredible journey and one that has made my dream come true: sharing the magic of Feng Shui with as many people around the world as possible. I couldn't have done it without the amazing people who have supported me along the way.

First and foremost, my family. To Patrick – thank you for your love, patience and the countless coffees that kept me going. Your unwavering belief in me, even when I doubted myself, means everything. And to Immy – thank you for being the most wonderful daughter I could wish for. Thank you for being so understanding on all the evenings I was tucked away writing and for reminding me to step away from my desk and have fun! You inspire me every day to show you that anything is possible.

To my incredible editor, Sophie, and the entire publishing team at Watkins – thank you for your guidance and expertise. And to Hannah, my literary agent – your belief in me and the power of Feng Shui made this possible.

To Amanda – thank you so much for your incredible insights and expertise.

Victoria, Ange and Kirst – thank you for everything. This book would not have happened without all your support behind the scenes.

Lucie – thank you for believing in me right from the beginning!

And finally, to my wonderful community – thank you for your support, messages and the trust you place in my work. You are the reason I do what I do, and I am so, so grateful.

INDEX

ABOUT THE AUTHOR

Kimberley Gallagher is a modern Feng Shui expert and founder of The Feng Shui Flow, where she combines classical Feng Shui principles with neuroscience, design psychology and intentional living. Through her warm, down-to-earth approach, Kimberley has helped thousands of women around the world bring more calm, clarity and abundance into their homes and their lives. Her work blends ancient wisdom with modern practicality, making Feng Shui feel less intimidating and more empowering. She is also the creator of the So Much Love community and the Feng Shui Flow Practitioner Course, which trains the next generation of home-energy experts. *The Calm and Happy Home* is her first book.